IT'S YOUR FUNERAL

JOHN PARRY

This book will
save you money on
funeral arranging

ISBN 978-1-909121-88-1

Acorn Independent Press

Sooner or later, you will need to arrange a suitable send off for someone. The sobering reality of arranging (and paying) for your funeral can be significantly reduced. This 'no holds barred' guide examines the mind-boggling power that funeral directors have over individuals from every walk of life, including their own staff.

Written from the industry coalface, it cuts through:

- The secrets that shroud the funeral trade.
- The common myths and perceptions that people have about funerals.
- All the common pitfalls when arranging a funeral.

This is your 360 degree window into a fascinating profession.

John has worked within the funeral industry for over 10 years and has "seen it all" when it comes to how independently run funeral homes and national companies operate in a highly competitive world.

During his career, John has had a ringside seat in terms of observing vulnerable and bereaved families at the hands of funeral arrangers, determined to reach their revenue targets. Some resort to unscrupulous methods that are mostly hidden from the average family at the time of need.

John is determined to raise the bar when it comes to professionalism within the industry through fair pricing, embalming standards and providing families with a first class funeral service.

If some funeral directors feel offended by some of the revelations contained within this book, John Parry makes no apology for attempting to draw attention to what is currently a tarnished, but only occasionally corrupt industry.

Contents

PART 1: THE INDUSTRY

Chapter 1: The Tradition of a Funeral 11

Chapter 2: Before Approaching a Funeral Director 14

Chapter 3: What to Expect at the Funeral Home
           & How it All Works 16

Chapter 4: Mark-ups That Will Shock You 30

Chapter 5: How to Choose a Funeral Director 35

PART 2: YOUR CHOICES

Chapter 6: Choosing a Crematorium 45

Chapter 7: Choosing a Cemetery or Catacomb 53

Chapter 8: Choosing a Stonemason 60

Chapter 9: Choosing a Florist 65

Chapter 10: Choosing a Minister or Celebrant 70

Chapter 11: Choosing an Appropriate Coffin or Casket 79

Chapter 12: Choosing a Mode of Transport 84

Chapter 13: Embalming. Is it Really Necessary? 90

Chapter 14: The Chapel of Rest – to View or Not to View 96

Chapter 15: Planning a Wake 99

Chapter 16: Religious Beliefs and Funeral Styles 102

PART 3: LOGISTICS & LEGALITIES

Chapter 17: The Removal and Transportation of a Body 111

Chapter 18: Doctor's Fees (Ash Cash)...114

Chapter 19: The Coroner 118

Chapter 20: The State Funeral (Pauper's Funeral)
                      & Bereavement Payments...121

Chapter 21: The Importance of Making a Will 124

Chapter 22: Probate 127

Chapter 23: Pre-paid Funeral Planning 130

Chapter 24: Repatriation 135

Chapter 25: Exhumation 137

PART 4: THE FINAL FAREWELL

Chapter 26: The Service, or 'Final Event' of a Loved One's Life.....143

Chapter 27: Ways to Enhance a Funeral Service................................148

Chapter 28: Bereavement Counselling and the
                      Truth About Tranquillizers..153

PART 5: FUNERAL FACTS

Chapter 29: Factual Anecdotes and Monumental Cock-ups 161

Chapter 30: Why the Funeral Industry is Preparing
                      for a Surge in the Death Rate..168

Chapter 31: Anatomical Facts & Funeral Statistics 170

Glossary of Terms 171

Image accreditations and special thanks: 172

Forms 173

PART 1

THE INDUSTRY

Chapter 1

The Tradition of a Funeral

People are always curious about their own existence. We continually re-assess our lives in detail as we strive to reach our ambitions and create comfortable, healthy lifestyles. Knowing there is no immortality leads us to ponder an uncomfortable question: "How long are we likely to live for?" Most people hope for a swift, painless end as they sleep when their time comes.

The aftermath of dying leaves our loved ones grieving and having to deal with our disposal fees. The demand for funerals is endless and overpricing is rife. Money may not be at the forefront of your mind in terms of grief, but if you don't try and cut some of these costs, you will be truly shocked when you receive the funeral bill.

The funeral industry ranks top when it comes to so-called brilliant, entrepreneurial achievements. Not only is it regarded as one of the world's oldest trades, but it is fast becoming one of the most lucrative markets.

Funeral ceremonies are probably as old as human culture itself. The earliest known example of a funeral ceremony was found in the Skhul cave at Qafzeh in Israel, dating back more than 100,000 years. The skeletal remains were covered in red ochre, with the jawbone of a wild boar placed alongside. Many other intriguing examples have been discovered all over the world after this period.

Today, funerals are mainly about providing a ceremony for celebrating, respecting, sanctifying and remembering the life of someone that has died. There are many complex beliefs involving funeral customs and how the dead are interred, or remembered through monuments and prayers.

Most youngsters have little consideration for the concept of dying and try to live their lives free of worry. They do not consider their own mortality until they lose someone close to them unexpectedly. The inevitability of death motivates people to turn to cultural beliefs that give their lives meaning and significance. By retirement age people are more likely to consider preparing for their own funerals (refer to chapter 24 Pre-paid Funeral Planning).

The process of dying involves complex chemistry. Its function produces an efficient sequence for the entire process of decomposition (refer to chapter 14 Embalming: Is It Really Necessary?). It involves *autolysis*; the breaking down of tissue matter through the body's own chemicals, and *putrefaction*; the breakdown of tissues through bacteria. The decomposition process of tissues must occur in order to prevent our environment from becoming a poisonous, pathogenic reservoir of bacteria. This provided an opportunity for entrepreneurial gain: charging for a ceremony and charging for the disposal of the body.

From the earliest Pagan funerals, the industry has now created its own extraordinary allegory that is packed with surprises, moral issues and frequent tales of woe.

The funeral business has now developed many facets and associated markets with a multi-billion pound turnover.

The industry has unsurprising predictability within its own market dynamics, and yet remains misunderstood or taboo for most individuals. It even has the potential to offer sustainable careers for thousands of school-leavers who are rarely informed about such obvious work specialities. Instead, their career advisers encourage other vocations where they can train in more classical and traditional middle class 'job for life' domains. The reality is that law; banking; nursing; civil service and engineering are all either cyclical, or subject to the laws of economics and government cuts. Market forces determine boom and bust, but few things are as steady and predictable as death. From the moment a person is born, an unknown date will mark their eventual death. For some people death is only moments away. For others, it could be several years, and for the really optimistic among us, death may be decades away.

Planning for the inevitable remains taboo.

Chapter 2

Before Approaching a Funeral Director

The time after a death can be confusing and overwhelming. This chapter outlines what you need to have done before you go to a funeral director.

Practicalities: What you need to do after a death has occurred

Step 1. Obtain a medical certificate from a GP or hospital doctor. However, it can only be issued if the doctor in question knows the cause of death and has been treating the deceased for the illness within the last 14 days. The medical certificate is required to register the death.

Step 2. You must register the death within five calendar days of death at a registrar's office, preferably nearest to where the death occurred. Any relative, somebody present at the time of death, an administrator from the hospital, or the person making the funeral arrangements is allowed to register a death.

An appointment with the registrar takes about half an hour and you will need:

- The medical certificate (signed by the doctor)
- The deceased's birth or marriage certificate
- The deceased's NHS medical card

The registrar will ask:

- The full name of the deceased when the death occurred
- Maiden name, if applicable
- The deceased's date of birth, and place of birth
- Their address
- Their occupation
- The full name, date of birth and occupation of their surviving partner
- Whether they were in receipt of a state pension, or any other benefits

Documents you will receive from the registrar:

- A certificate for burial or cremation. This is a green square form that gives permission for a burial or cremation to take place (known as "the green").
- A death certificate (extra copies can be purchased for a nominal fee).

You need to organise these documents before you can approach a funeral director.

Chapter 3

What to Expect at the Funeral Home & How it All Works

"The only thing we fear is old age... and a funeral director."

Roles: Who Does What?

Most funeral homes appear austere, forbidding and definitely the one place on the high street to avoid at all costs, until the death of a loved one has occurred. It can be useful to have a rough idea of who does what within the funeral home so that you understand the process. Hierarchy within an average funeral home generally falls into three organisational layers which, to the outside world, appear cold and veiled. The hierarchy covers:

1. The funeral director, conductors, a foreman and managers
2. Funeral arrangers and an accounts department
3. Embalmers, drivers, bearers and coffin makers

School leavers joining a medium to large-sized funeral home would hardly notice any difference had they joined the Army as a new recruit. Entering the business at ground level requires a period of acclimatisation where mandatory shiftwork becomes the norm. And 'callouts', or the retrieval of a body, can occur at any time of the day, or night. Early starts are standard practice, and any garage, or back office personnel are expected to be in their 'blacks' and ready to start the day shift by 8a.m. All under the watchful eye of a foreman.

When funeral work is at its busiest, the first hour of the day is extremely hectic whilst all staff prepare themselves for the day.

The smell of shoe polish lingers continuously as everyone attempts to show willing, and proving they are, at least, in work mode. Cars are prepped and polished with meticulous care by their drivers as they await their daily work schedules. The coffin maker begins working through the myriad of coffin sizes and styles from a new daily list, attaching plastic brass effect handles to the cremation coffins, and stapling clinically white cremfilm linings around the coffin interior to prevent leakage. It is the coffin maker's responsibility to ensure that each coffin fits the deceased accordingly. A trained coffin maker would know from experience precisely what size coffin to use without needing to refer to the imperial sizes attached to his work list. This is important because nobody would want to view their loved ones lying in an ill-fitting box. The interior linings must be finished neatly and correctly to give the impression that the deceased is at rest in the most comfortable surroundings. Although the handles for a cremation coffin are plastic and will never be used for carrying, they must be attached level and professionally. Finally, the coffin maker attaches the nameplate of someone's beloved husband, wife, son, or daughter onto the coffin lid. Coffin makers also report to the funeral director about stock levels.

Anyone caught slacking, or turning up late for work is the most likely candidate to take the hoover on its daily tour through the arranging rooms, corridors, chapels of rest and anywhere else where a client could potentially visit.

The Funeral Director

The funeral director, or person whose business it is to arrange the cremation or burial of the dead, is ultimately responsible for the smooth running of every funeral that leaves the premises, ensuring that the company has enough vehicles available to accommodate the daily workload, as well as organising each member of staff. Anyone running late, or who is absent through sick leave, will inevitably mess everything up logistically during the planning of daily funerals – they will need to make a very convincing case directly to their funeral director.

Vanloads of exhausted florists arrive at the funeral home every day. They deliver the floral tributes that have been painstakingly laboured over during the early hours for their clients.

By 9a.m. the front doors are unlocked to the world and the funeral home is ready for business. The funeral director, or senior members of staff, will firstly contact all the local crematoria to check the availability of time slots, and to confirm funeral times for any new arrangements. Each crematorium will have several funeral directors contacting them throughout the day as each company plans ahead for the next fortnight. It is crucial for funeral directors to offer primetime slots to their clients, predominantly between midday and 2p.m., if they are able to. By making en-bloc advance bookings to secure time slots (even in the absence of real clients), the funeral director creates greater flexibility for when genuine clients materialise. And the funeral director certainly hopes they materialise in abundance. En-bloc bookings are an old tactic used by funeral directors at the start of the week, which ultimately creates an unfair logistical nightmare for their competitors, as well as crematoria management.

Booking peak cremation time slots could become a thing of the past for family-run independents and the Co-operative Funeralcare hubs as the Dignity funeral homes often own the crematoria. The Dignity Group own about 35 crematoria and are likely to continue acquiring more, or building new ones within areas where their own funeral homes are well-established. However, the Co-operative now own several in the north of England and in Scotland.

The Conductor, aka 'Manager'

Within a medium to large size funeral organisation, becoming a conductor is often perceived to be the most prestigious position for any employee of long term standing to aspire to. This is because the conductor has a principal role, and one that is highly revered, but it is also regarded as the easiest aspect of the entire funeral!

Nevertheless, there is a world of difference between those individuals who conduct their funeral ceremonies with pride, and those that adopt a more casual approach. The conducting staff within family-run independents generally appear better organised and more dedicated than many conductors from national organisations.

The role of the 'front man' goes way beyond basic grooming and general etiquette. Earning the respect of their colleagues and the people working with them is just as important as earning the respect of their clients. Without hard earned respect no one bothers to work as a team, and if things go wrong, the conductor will suddenly feel quite alone. The conductor ensures that every detail requested by the family is carried through. This includes:

1. Liaising with the funeral director about timings and transport arrangements.
2. Ensuring all cremation and burial forms are correct and delivered on time.
3. Checking final arrangements with clients and dealing with any jewellery requests.
4. Handling donation collections.
5. Laying out floral tributes and returning floral cards.
6. Greeting ministers and paying ministers' fees.
7. Arranging seating protocol.
8. Issuing orders of service.
9. Organising an attachment of staff.
10. Organising picking up and dropping off points.

The Foreman

The foreman, or 'general manager in charge', is not usually a popular role.

At its best, the position is attained by a member of staff with plenty of experience and know-how for when things go disastrously wrong. Running a funeral business is often about knowing whom to contact when things have not gone to plan. Foremen are also tasked to diffuse petty disputes, or discipline staff whenever they get out of line. When adverse situations are handled professionally, it will earn the foreman a revered reputation and appreciation.

At its worst, the feeling of power becomes all too enjoyable for the foreman with an oversized ego, who typically becomes the funeral directors 'agent of filth', attracting resentment among the ranks. Truths and mistruths will feed through to the top with snide and precision, about whomever had dared to cross the worst kind of foreman's path.

The upside for the funeral director is that most of the staff end up towing the line for the sake of a quiet life. However, watching employees fawning over their 'agent of filth', breaking each other's arms to pour his coffee each morning in the process, must certainly be satisfying entertainment for the funeral director that enjoys observing their anathema.

The Funeral Arranger

First impressions count, and the entire process of reassuring a family that they have found the right company to care for their loved one hinges on the funeral arranger's attitude, mannerisms and ability to build good rapport. Their role is the first of the three stages within the entire funeral process, and finding a good arranger is crucial for the smooth running of any funeral business.

The ideal arranger will be: of smart appearance; well groomed; confident and knowledgeable; everyone's friend; a team player; well organised and a persuasive negotiator. Over time many have become avid bookworms or even take up the odd sideline hobby to help them get through the long, uneventful periods when nothing happens.

The Embalmer

Assuming that a funeral director has decided that embalming the deceased is a necessary and important aspect of the business (a few do not), then some of the firm's staff will be trained in mortuary care. Embalming courses are hugely expensive and a funeral director will consider, very carefully, the merits of sending a member of his staff off to an embalming college for at least two years. Firstly, the individual may not pass all the necessary modules. Secondly, they become more employable with an embalming qualification and might decide to work elsewhere.

The embalmer will keep an organised bank of fridges with details of each deceased carefully logged with corresponding identity tags attached to the wrist or ankle. Whenever an identity tag has accidentally fallen off during transit from a hospital, care home, nursing home, or the deceased's home, it is the responsibility of the embalmer to replace it. This must stay with the deceased at all times to prevent mistakes from happening.

Alternatively, a funeral director may decide to call upon the services of a self-employed 'trade embalmer'. However, the promise of an embalming qualification provides an excellent carrot for a funeral director to offer anyone during the recruitment process because it will be perceived as an opportunity to progress and prosper within the company.

Bearers and Drivers

These staff members are often affectionately referred to as 'back room boys'. Because of the general nature of their work, they have to be fit, of an average height of six foot, and are therefore predominantly male. Their work is on call with the opportunity to earn overtime (which is probably just as well). Bearers are trained in the handling of coffins and caskets prior to a cremation service, as well as any graveside burial arrangement. They must also learn all aspects of limousine and hearse driving etiquette. Whilst on call they must be prepared to collect a deceased person from a care home, a hospital mortuary, a coroner's office, or from any private address. Collections can be challenging because the on-call staff may not know how large the deceased person is, or the circumstances of how they met their death. This work is not for the faint-hearted, and each bearer and driver will have to work hard over the years, in the hope that one day they may be promoted to the position of conductor. Waiting for the 'dead man's shoes' position becomes a way of life and becomes all too elusive for most.

For the thousands of men and women that work in funeral homes, the environment becomes addictive. Staff that had initially arrived for a fleeting six-month temporary job soon realise how comfortable life can become working within an ancient profession, and they establish themselves as part of the furniture.

The trick for fresh recruits is to find the ultimate funeral home with the ideal working environment. Get it right and the daily routine becomes pleasurable. Returning to base at the end of a long day and being greeted by the company's doe eyed, friendly receptionist creates a decompression chamber of laughter and banter. Get it wrong and the office remains a cold, unsympathetic treadmill.

The workforce that make up the 'necessary staff' orchestrate every funeral that leaves the funeral home. They are uniquely loyal, and by virtue of the nature of the funeral industry are, virtually guaranteed a job for life. Whether they are employed as a driver; bearer; coffin maker; conductor, or a combination of each, their job functions will remain unchanged and sustainable. So long as they are able to work alongside each other, as part of a disciplined, punctual team, they are expected to develop a working camaraderie.

This will always be of great comfort to them, knowing they will have the support of colleagues that have learnt to adapt and cope with a less than substantial salary during their careers.

(NB. Bearers appreciate a tip).

What Will Happen When You Step Into a Funeral Home?

From the moment you are greeted inside a funeral home, the arranger will assess your ability to pay and how much you are likely to spend before the selling begins. An appointment for your initial visit will not be necessary, and for most people it will be a strange experience.

A smartly-dressed receptionist or uniformed member of the undertaker's staff will greet you with a well-trained expression of warmth and compassion. They will appear sincere, humbled and saddened by your loss as you begin to explain whom you are arranging the funeral for, or that doctors have recently informed you that the death of your loved one is now imminent. An open palm beckoning you towards the privacy of an arranging room will have gone unnoticed.

The array of comfortable chairs around a central coffee table will provide ample and relaxed seating for you to discuss the personal details, and you will be made to feel very much at home. A box of tissues will be within easy reach in case you are overcome by an outpouring of grief. There will be no need to feel awkward about your emotions as the staff have heard similar tales to yours before, and many times over. Someone's mother or father that had been taken into care umpteen years ago when dementia, or Alzheimer's disease became unmanageable; the wife or husband that died on the journey to work due to heart failure; the son who took his own life after a tiff with a girlfriend; or the lad who lost his life after coming off his cherished motorbike.

However tragic or unfortunate the circumstances of your loss, the arranger will have undoubtedly encountered a similar scenario, and depending on their years of service, they would have become de-sensitised to any scenario concerning death long ago. In a busy funeral home, there typically might be hundreds, if not thousands, of bodies passing through its mortuary in any given year.

At first, the funeral director (or arranger) will simply listen attentively to your situation, and then it's straight down to business. The two of you will now sit alone with the door closed, indicating to other members of staff that you are not to be disturbed. Funeral directors use their own language when in client mode. A fatal accident broadcast through national media is designed to capture the interests of a mass audience, and words such as, "death" or "died" are the accepted format. In a funeral home these words are rarely bandied about to the public. Instead euphemisms such as "passed away" are used to create a softer impact.

You are then asked a series of standard, personalised questions without reference to your loved one, so that a funeral bill can be established.

"Would you prefer Dad (or Mum) to be cremated or buried?"
"Are there any other family members living close by, or will they all be travelling from afar?"

"How many people are you expecting to attend the funeral?"
"Where is Dad (or Mum) now?"
"What was the name of the doctor that issued the certificate of death?"
"Was Dad (or Mum) fitted with a pacemaker or defibrillator?"
"Is Dad (or Mum) wearing any jewellery?"

The phrasing of each question has psychology that helps to create a purpose of care, and everyone wants to feel that their loved ones are being cared for.

Sooner or later you will gaze at several 'point of sale' objects carefully displayed around the room. A distinguished photo of a black funeral carriage drawn by a pair of Friesian horses and its deadpan coachman peer down at you from a wall mounting. Other pictures may include photos of a proud funeral director, or conductor in action, marching in front of a hearse, wearing a classic, heavy frock coat, top hat and cane. Some manage it quite well and carry a natural air of grandeur and panache, whilst others appear disorganised with ill-fitting, threadbare attire, and their attitudes seemingly 'wide boy'. Others spend their careers emulating a second-rate gameshow host.

As you are invited to select a coffin from a glossy brochure, you remain unaware of the phenomenal price increases brought by each turn of the page.

Top tip: Because over 70% of all funerals are cremations, the coffin will be presented for a maximum of 40 minutes. It will then be cremated along with your loved one. In reality only a basic coffin is required because its value will completely go up in smoke within an hour or two of the funeral.

Then once you have decided on the coffin comes the question: "How many people are you expecting to attend the funeral?"

The reasons for asking this question are twofold. Firstly, your funeral arranger will need to determine the size of chapel to book, and secondly, to calculate how many limousines to sell you. Each limousine is designed to carry six mourners. It will not matter if the funeral home that you have selected only owns one or two vehicles because they will arrange to hire additional vehicles from other funeral homes, at a considerable cost to you.

If you opt for a horse-drawn funeral, make sure that you have not been charged for the cost of a hearse as well. Mistakes can, and often do, happen.

At this stage of the meeting, you will find yourself alone for a few minutes whilst your arranger checks availability of time slots. Uppermost in your mind is your own personal grief and vulnerability. But you will also be thankful that a knowledgeable and friendly expert has now taken care of a matter that you know so little about.

Perhaps you begin to consider your own mortality for the first time because someone close to you has just passed away. You will not fail to miss sensitively written leaflets offering will writing services and, of course, literature about pre-paid funeral planning for you to take away (refer to Chapter 22: The Importance of Making a Will, and Chapter 24: Pre-paid Funeral Planning).

When your arranger returns to confirm the details of the funeral times, you will also receive a total package of costs breaking down the funeral director's professional fees.

These will include: an allowance for organising legal documentation such as cremation papers, the allocation of necessary staff, hygienic treatment (embalming), the grade or type of coffin, type of hearse and number of limousines required. It will also include third party costs. The three basic third party costs are additional fees beyond the control of the funeral director, but have to be included in an overall package of costs. They are:

1. The crematorium or cemetery fees.
2. Doctors' fees (cremations only).
3. The minister's or celebrant's fee.

These are the just the basic third party costs, but there are many other potential third party costs depending on how lavish the funeral arrangements become. For example: a horse-drawn funeral, a choir, a web cast recording, digging fees for a woodland burial, a Scottish bagpiper, a dove release, etc.

After you have been presented with the costs, a practical question about money soon follows: "Was a funeral plan taken out to cover the costs?"

In reality the arranger knows that this is unlikely, because setting money aside to pay for a funeral is generally low on the priority list. Those who do want to make some kind of funeral plan often find that their family find it too upsetting to discuss and so plans get sidelined. For more information on pre-paid funeral plans see Chapter 24.

However, the arranger has cemented the seed for purchasing and organising one at a later date. It becomes a subtle selling tool that funeral directors know will be of benefit to every family.

Any funeral plan that has been properly underwritten is worth its weight in gold and will save your family thousands of pounds, particularly when they are not needed for several years. However, even with a funeral plan in place there may be shortfalls and additional disbursement costs that are not covered by the insurance plan. These will be charged for at the time of need, at a higher cost than previously quoted for.

Next comes the question of religion: "What faith, if any, did (name) follow?"

Whichever religion or faith you decide is most befitting for your loved one, the funeral director will be running through a mental list of ministers for that faith that he will later contact to check their availability, and to officiate the funeral service (refer to Chapter 11: Choosing A Minister or Celebrant).

You will then receive your arrangement folder confirming the price; a standardised 'thank you for entrusting our company and using our services for (deceased's name) funeral, etc.' letter; the address of where you need to register the deceased; advice about expensive ways to dispose of your loved one's ashes, and without fail – a leaflet about will writing and pre-paid funeral planning.

You will either leave the premises relieved that your loved one is finally in the safe hands of an expert or questioning the arranger's integrity and wondering if you really have received value for money. Under normal circumstances 'buyer's remorse' can be dealt with by way of refund within a standard period of time. The same principle applies with a funeral arrangement, *even if you have handed over a hefty deposit* and agreed to allow a company to proceed with arranging a funeral. Although time is limited to cancel a funeral arrangement, it is, within reason, still possible.

Beware: entrusting a funeral director to perform any funeral service can become their licence to print money.

Chapter 4

Mark-ups That Will Shock You

Wherever you decide to go for the arrangement of your loved one's funeral, the final funeral bill or quote, when totalled, should contain a comprehensive package of costs combining the professional services of the funeral director and any third party costs.

Here is an example of how the funeral costs are broken down:

INVOICE NO: xxxxx   **Date: 1st January 20xx**

To: AN Other
     Any Town

Professional fees:

To make all legal arrangements for the cremation of AN Other Snr. at Reading Crematorium, Monday 12th January 4p.m.; to supply a peaceful chapel of rest and the provision of necessary staff

	£ 1500.00
Hygienic treatment	**£ 150.00**
To supply a black carriage hearse & two horses	**£ 1200.00**
The provision of two limousines	**£ 550.00**
Third party fees:	
Crematorium fees	**£ 749.00**
Doctor's fees	**£ 162.00**
Minister's fees	**£ 190.00**

Total: **£4,501.00**
Thank you for entrusting us to take care of the funeral arrangements
Terms: Payment is due 14 days after the funeral

All costings are derived from a menu of services that you must scrutinise thoroughly if you are to succeed in reducing your funeral quotation. When the final bill is presented to you there may be one or two surprising additional extras, such as: the viewing fee for visiting your loved one during your visit to the chapel of rest over the period preceding the funeral. This depends entirely on the policy of each individual funeral home.

Unsurprisingly, the majority of people do not bother. They usually walk away, reasoning that the final amount must be correct. The psychology of funeral arranging is beyond compare due to all the emotions involved. People are understandably in a depressed and vulnerable state when they lose someone close to them. They are grateful that someone else has now taken responsibility for the care of a loved one, and naturally only want the best for them.

A typical funeral business would mark up their most basic coffin to retail at least six times what they pay for it. When a client chooses a mid to top range coffin, the purchase is nearly always down to emotional pride. With a few modifications here and there and a fresh coat of varnish, the final retail value suddenly increases by up to 30 fold.

A limousine will accommodate up to six mourners and should guarantee its passengers a smooth, comfortable ride, completing an average return journey of approximately 12 miles. Each vehicle that is hired will represent approximately 15 per cent of your total bill.

Top tip: Ask any able family member, including friends of the family who wish to attend the funeral, to drive themselves to the venue.

Horse-drawn hearses are majestic, graceful and eye-catching. They were the original mode of funeral transport, long before the introduction of any motorised vehicles during the early 1920s. As the roads became busier with automation, it became cheaper and quicker to transport the deceased by motorised hearse. These days horse-drawn carriages are making a welcome revival (refer to Chapter 13: Choosing the Mode of Transport). But as resplendent as they are, they are expensive.

Cremated remains caskets are about the size of a shoebox and resemble a small casket. They are a much more palatable way of receiving your loved one's ashes and aesthetically more presentable than the standard plastic containers that are supplied by the local crematoriums. Your funeral director will mark these up by approximately eight fold (assuming he has not received a quantity of caskets free of charge from his coffin supplier for buying coffins in bulk).

The hygienic treatment (aka embalming) of the deceased will involve a range of specialist chemicals; cold cosmetics and the embalmer's labour. The mark-up to you will be approximately 40 per cent (sometimes whether you want the service or not).

The removal of the deceased from where they have died usually requires two members of staff, a plastic or fibre glass transporting shell to carry the deceased during a removal, a van and some fuel. The mark-up to you will be approximately 120 per cent if the funeral home is within your locality. Long distance removal costs will be significantly higher.

Families are encouraged to have an order of service compiled containing photographs and content details of the service. The cost of printing and production are negligible but a funeral home could mark up their production costs by as much as 200 per cent.

Funerals are now multi-level businesses. Funeral arrangers are employed to sell you funeral products and are targeted to specifically sell you as much as possible.

To openly query the frugality of a grieving family with a response such as "Don't you want the best?" is a tad too blunt, even for an inexperienced arranger to get away with. Instead, they painstakingly guide and explain all the merits of booking as many additional items as possible. The chances are that you will want that additional limousine, or oak-panelled coffin for a deservingly opulent send-off.

Just remember that within a couple of miles of receiving your quote for funeral services there will be another funeral director who will be determined to offer a cheaper quote, particularly when they are competing with the national chains.

- Funeral quotes vary considerably from one funeral home to another
- Every item written within the funeral director services has a negotiable cost
- Every funeral has fixed 'third party' costs that are non-negotiable

Chapter 5

How to Choose a Funeral Director

Types of Funeral Directors

There are approximately 4,800 funeral homes throughout the United Kingdom and they are divided into three groups: Dignity plc.; Co-operative Funeralcare, and independent funeral directors. Approximate breakdowns are:

600 are owned by Dignity plc.

1200 are owned by Co-operative Funeralcare

3000 are owned by independent funeral directors

Over time, independents have learnt to live alongside their Co-operative Funeralcare competitors whilst keeping an aloof distance from any Co-op staff. And yet both groups tend to view the American Dignity funeral homes with caution and a degree of disdain for the way they are set up and how they operate. In 2009, Co-operative Funeralcare became the first ever funeral company to launch a national television campaign. But by 2012 they featured on the Channel 4 *Dispatches* programme *Undercover Undertaker,* after an investigator secretly filmed behind the scenes.

How to Choose a Funeral Director

With so much choice, it can be hard to know where to start. The most important thing to remember is not to rush into anything too soon. Just because your loved one has passed away does not necessarily mean that everything has to be booked and dealt with immediately. Do as much research as possible in the first instance and discuss various options with other family members and consider an affordable working budget.

All types of funeral directors will market their services. This ranges from adverts and websites to talks at local care homes, nursing homes and hospitals. However, there may be some local funeral directors that you have not heard of so do some research.

* Word of Mouth

This is often the soundest form of recommendation, but if it has come from a healthcare professional it may not be unbiased advice. More proactive funeral directors arrange seminars or become part of the in-house staff training at local residential care homes, nursing homes and hospitals. Their training programmes are entitled *When a Death Occurs* and are designed specifically to spark anecdotal debate, and unravel myriad of myths that cloud the funeral profession. It is the funeral director's golden opportunity to impress the managers of the care homes, etc. and their staff by talking creatively and knowledgeably about their profession. In return, the services of the funeral director will be recommended to the residents' families when their time of need comes.

More reliable word of mouth may be asking friends and family if they have attended any professional and dignified funerals in the local area.

- Your Local Crematorium's Attendant

Crematoria and cemeteries can accommodate approximately 12 cremation funerals or burials a day, five days a week. Once a family has entered the private solemnity of a chapel, they are seated for the beginning of their farewells to a loved one, whilst a world of activity is unleashed in another room.

After each floral tribute has been removed from the hearse and positioned around the viewing terrace, the person in charge in the attendant's office becomes occupied by bearers, drivers and a funeral conductor who will only gain about 15 minutes of the attendant's undivided attention. His office is now a conduit for rumours, anecdotes and general gossip, including all the latest 'jaw dropping' and 'world shattering' hot industry news. This is where careers are made, cut short and even vanquished. It is also where competitive pricing can flourish or be destroyed.

With the entry music now playing, and the minister in action behind the lectern, the attendant is now free to listen, dissect and interject with every piece of gossip, or news of a local interest.

"Well?" is an uncomplicated cue for any whisperings to commence.

The lads naively perform their roles as marketeers, excitedly regurgitating the flawless syntax of a well-aimed pricing war. Any business model devised beforehand by the funeral director will temporarily unsettle the competition. Within minutes, and at zero cost, the team activate an entire marketing strategy whilst overseeing the family within the chapel.

The conversation will end as quickly as it had started and attention focuses on the immediate needs of the family members. The funeral staff return to their cars and are ready to ferry people away to a nearby pub or back to their homes. Within minutes the attendant plays host to the next attachment of funeral staff, falling over everyone with enthusiasm as they pass on the next layers of news. News flies around the funeral industry faster and often more effectively than any form of social media, as intended.

And of course the more powerful the content of the bearers' news, the more it will hold the attendant's attention. For instance, the dismissal of an undertaker's key employee for renting out the company fleet for evening limousine hire, or the latest firm in court for negligence.

So the next time you attend someone's funeral and the minister announces a piece of music for reflection, committal or as the chosen exit song – and nothing happens... rest assured that the news being measured out in the side room will be far more interesting at that precise moment than the minister's cue for music. Music cues are frequently missed, but if your sense of humour has not totally abandoned you, then the expression of angst and agitated hand gesturing at the lectern is likely to be as comical as any *Fawlty Towers* sketch.

Top tip: Visit your local crematoriums and chapels for a friendly chat with the chapel attendants when they are quiet. You may discover the best deals and which companies are the easiest ones to deal with. Attendants always have their ear to the ground, and will be only too pleased to tell you everything they know.

• Trade Associations

Trade associations are a good place to look because members must adhere to very professional codes of practices. They produce heavy manuals advising on best practice in all elements of funeral arranging. Below are a few:

1. The National Association of Funeral Directors (NAFD) was established in 1905 and represents a large proportion of the funeral industry. Their purpose is to ensure that

their members maintain a high code of conduct at all times and they also provide quality training programmes.

The NAFD also run an online obituary service called Forever Online. This is a free online obituary service that enables bereaved families to inform a wide circle of friends and relatives about the death of a loved one.

The industry standard qualifications in funeral directing are those organised by the NAFD.

Other trade associations include:

2. The British Institute of Funeral Directors (BIFD). This was established in 1982 with the purpose of promoting best practice through learning.

3. The Society of Allied and Independent Funeral Directors (SAIF) was established in 1989, whose (approximately) 700 members are all independent funeral directors. Their purpose is to promote and protect their group of independent funeral directors.

4. The National Association of Pre-paid Funeral Plans (NAPFP) (refer to Chapter 24: Pre-paid Funeral Planning)

By becoming a member of the NAFD, a funeral director will be bound by the association's rules and codes of conduct to some degree, but not every company feels the same necessity to join. In fact, 15% do not.

5. The National Federation of Funeral Directors (NFFD) was set up in 2010 and offers its members a completely new approach to funeral directing. An ancient industry is bound to be adverse to change, particularly when a

new association offers its members a radically modern alternative with highly competitive pricing. The NFFD are only interested in attracting new members that are prepared to promote transparency; increase value for money, and streamline working practices. If practiced wisely, the philosophy should ultimately be of benefit to the industry and the consumer. The overriding message from the NFFD and its members is to "give the customer what they want, at a price they can afford". Their input has been instrumental in the development of SafeHands funeral plans, which are becoming the UK's fastest growing pre-paid funeral plan provider. By carefully monitoring the funeral plan market and scrutinising the business models of their competitors, and recognising their deficiencies, they claim to have devised newer and more transparent ways to operate. They were also the first funeral plan provider to advertise their products on national television.

Their business interests also extend to Funeralstore: www.funeralstore.co.uk, who are the UK's leading provider of heavily-discounted funeral and mortuary equipment. They also own and operate www.candlememorials.com. This facility allows a bereaved consumer to leave a lasting tribute in memorandum of a lost loved one.

Shop Around

A word to the wise: shop around, then shop around again. There really is no immediate hurry! Shop around to compare quotes. There is usually more than one funeral director in town. If you were purchasing a new car, you would definitely shop around and not just accept the first quote. So why should a funeral be any different?

Every town has its own average benchmark for funeral pricing, and every now and then, a new (or non-established undertaker) attempts the unthinkable by competing against the benchmark price. Pricing is calculated by the larger, well-established companies to offset their higher running costs and overheads. Larger companies have additional employees to pay for, as well as the maintenance of a larger fleet of vehicles.

Imagine their frustration and irritation when each carefully-planned rumour goes around that AN Other Funeral Director is offering a basic funeral package at a snip. It is incredibly easy to put the word out. Throughout each working day, all around the country, rumours and gossip are circulated throughout the industry. Every year, when new annual price lists are calculated, funeral directors deploy several tactics to obtain each other's newly-calculated funeral packages in the same way that other retailers do. These days a funeral director is constantly striving to maximise its profit margins through tactical methods.

Get quotes, name-drop and do not be afraid to mention prices already quoted. Funeral directors know their own margins and have a good idea of what their competitors are likely to be quoting.

Weighing Up The Quotes

Your comparative funeral quotations are likely to vary considerably, but just because one company is cheaper than another does not necessarily mean their standards are the same. Any funeral is only as good as how its staff perform on the day. Track records, word-of-mouth reviews and advice from trade associations may offer indications of standard.

If you already have a funeral director in mind, you still need to think carefully. When a person passes away from natural causes you may already have a funeral director in mind whom you would prefer to take care of all the arrangements. Your choice may be because of someone else's recommendation, or that your family had used the company in the past. There might even be a funeral plan written into the deceased's will stating a preference.

Top tip: Take care when making arrangements with a funeral company. A loved one may have specified a particular funeral home. However, that may have since been taken over by another company.

The American company Dignity are now wise to some adverse perceptions about them operating their businesses within local communities. They ensure that the majority of people remain unaware that the old family that ran the business, whose name remains above the door (the name by which families are entrusting), have since sold out to Dignity. After all, it is in the interest of the new undertaker to capitalise from the hard work and reputation built up by the former undertaker (this also applies to larger independents when taking over a smaller firm). Usually once they are taken over, the prices go up.

PART 2

YOUR CHOICES

Chapter 6

Choosing a Crematorium

An Introduction to Crematoriums

The cremation of human remains dates back at least 20,000 years and an archaeological record exists of the 'Mungo Lady' which are the remains of a partly-cremated body found at Mungo Lake in Australia.

These days a cremation involves the use of high temperature burning, vaporisation and oxidation to reduce dead bodies to basic chemical compounds, such as gases and fragments of dry bone. They are usually attached to a chapel, and most offer an independent facility to the public.

The process involves a body with its coffin being burnt inside a cremator. Each crematorium will have one or more cremators that are able to generate temperatures of 870°C to 980°C. These high temperatures ensure that a corpse will disintegrate.

The concept of cremation funerals reached Britain from Italy after a model of cremation apparatus was exhibited at the Vienna Exposition in 1873, which attracted huge attention, including that of Sir Henry Thompson, a surgeon and physician to Queen Victoria. He promoted the concept enthusiastically on the grounds of sanitary precaution against the propagation of disease. He also believed cremations would prevent individuals being buried alive as well as reducing the cost of funerals. They also spared mourners the necessity of being exposed to the weather during interment, and urns would be safe from vandalism. On the 13th

January 1874, Sir Henry Thompson and his advocates founded the Cremation Society of Great Britain.

Cremations were not made legal in Britain before 1885, when the first crematorium was built in Woking. A surge in the demand for cremation funerals followed with the construction of new crematoria throughout Britain. Manchester had one by 1892; Glasgow by 1895; Liverpool by 1896; Hull, 1901; Leicester and Golders Green by 1902; Birmingham by 1903; and City of London by 1904.

Contrary to belief, cremators are designed to burn one body and its coffin at a time and each body is usually cremated within an hour of the service.

Many crematoria are having additional and larger cremators installed, as they prepare for the inevitable end of a generation of longevity (anticipated en masse 2015 onwards) and deaths caused from obesity. Standard cremators are constructed at 33 inches in width and cannot accommodate customised coffins that resemble double wardrobes.

How to Research Crematoriums

Many families that book a cremation funeral have no idea what standards they are likely to receive on the day of the funeral. The crematorium selected by the funeral director may not necessarily be the most suitable for you or your mourners. This may be down to simple logistics that only suit the funeral home. This is about what suits you and your family, not what suits the funeral home, so it is important to know where alternative crematoria are located, who manages them and how their prices compare.

Crematoria do not openly advertise themselves, and receive all their bookings from funeral directors.

Managing the gardens and grounds within any multi-acre site is very important and requires constant maintenance. But a privately run, or council-owned crematorium that lacks the necessary funds to employ enough grounds men may cause embarrassment on the day of the funeral. There is nothing more unsightly than seeing grass that has been left uncut for years just yards away from freshly-mown grass verges along the entire length of the driveway. Your guests may have travelled a long way and would expect to see the crematoria grounds in pristine condition.

It may be worthwhile also enquiring about other facilities that are available for your guests, such as:

- Is there a well-run cafeteria?
- Will there be a florist for any last minute floral requirements?
- How many waiting rooms and chapels are there?
- Do the waiting rooms have water dispensers?
- Is there any wheelchair access for disabled guests?
- How clean are the facilities?
- Are the chapels in a state of disrepair? When was the last time they were refurbished?

Further Choices and Decisions

A mixture of funeral jargon and traditional protocol can be confusing when deciding a suitable resting place for your loved one's cremated remains. Below are some extra things to think about.

Leaving the Ashes at the Crematorium

Deciding how to dispose of cremated remains is sometimes written into a will, or in the absence of a will, the person who had applied for the funeral. The final resting place for cremated remains is a personal choice and some crematoriums prefer any requests to be delivered in writing.

A 'committal of ashes' is where cremated remains are buried. Once buried they cannot be legally removed from the ground unless they are in a container and a licence has been obtained from the government.

Most crematoriums have memorial gardens or a cemetery where your loved ones ashes can be interred into a cremated remains plot, or into an existing family grave. Cremated remains plots are generally arranged in groups of four, consisting of small graves. Permission will be required from the named grave owner, and a burial fee will be charged by the crematorium.

Top tip: There is nothing preventing you from burying cremated remains in your own garden, without cost.

Most crematorium gardens are beautifully kept and offer tranquil and peaceful settings all year round. However, standards vary from being kept thoroughly pristine to being woefully neglected, with too few staff available to maintain their sizeable acreage.

Memorials & Plaques

Overall, staff at crematoria know how important it is for families to have a special place of their own when visiting a loved one, and offer a wide range of memorials, plaques, living memorials and stone memorials.

- The concept of purchasing a memorial within a garden of remembrance is no different from a cemetery or churchyard, except for the length of lease. Memorials within crematoriums are available for 10 years, and when they are not renewed, they will be offered to another family.
- Columbarium wall plaques are made of plastic or bronze and allow an inscription of up to 60 characters (including spaces), which are usually written across five lines. Slate plaques also allow 60 characters and are written across three lines by a stonemason. Name plates are attached horizontally to the front of the columbarium to commemorate a loved one.
- Floris plaques allow four lines of inscription with a maximum of 30 characters. It is possible to have a ceramic insert with a painted motif or photograph.
- Posy vases allow only two lines of inscription:

  The name of the deceased
  The year of birth and death

- Living memorials include trees and shrubs that are leased for 10-year terms, but never become your personal property. If the plant dies within the lease period it will be replaced and maintained by the crematorium garden staff.

- Stone memorials include: vase blocks, sanctum vaults and wall niches.
  - Vase blocks and sanctum vaults are sometimes made from pink granite or white marble surrounds. White marble memorials usually have a black or red tablet with gilt lettering but stain easily and are costly to replace (refer to Chapter 9: Choosing the Right Stonemason).
  - Sanctum vaults (designated spaces large enough for cremated remains to be interred) allow eight lines of inscription with some lines having up to 20 or 30 characters. Ceramic discs with a motif or a photograph can be purchased, and each vault holds up to two sets of cremated remains, although urn sizes are sometimes restricted. A special licence is required from the government if you want to take them elsewhere at a later date.
  - The larger wall niches hold up to four sets of cremated remains and the smaller ones hold up to two. The total amount of characters is restricted to basic details of the deceased and a licence is not required for the removal of an ashes container from a wall niche.
- Granite and wooden benches are another way of remembering a loved one and most benches have space for two name plaques. The quantity of benches in memorial gardens is often restricted because of aesthetic or budgetary reasons.
- A Hall of Remembrance can be found within a crematorium complex or in a separate building within the crematorium grounds. Some families choose to have an entry written into a book of remembrance as well as having other kinds of memorial. They are

skillfully-written and crafted with colourful emblems as a permanent memorial. Each contains an entry of two, five or eight lines that are written by professional calligraphers. The pages are turned daily to display the correct date.

Alternative Plans for the Ashes

If you prefer to keep the ashes at home or organise the committal elsewhere, you will need to decide what kind of container to use for the transportation of cremated remains. It is part of the funeral director's arrangements and responsibility to collect them for you, otherwise you may opt to collect them yourself.

Top tip: If a funeral director decides to make a charge for collecting cremated remains, there is nothing to stop you collecting them yourself. Funeral directors make regular trips to crematoria anyway to deliver paperwork and to conduct funerals. You should not be charged an additional fee for this service.

It may come as an unpalatable shock when collecting your loved one's cremated remains when they are handed to you in a plastic container known as a polytainer. Particularly if the funeral bill has already reached astronomical proportions. There are a variety of alternative containers available – at a price.

Biodegradable containers are available for the interring of ashes at a churchyard, or a wooden casket (or urn) can be purchased either directly from a crematorium, or from a funeral director. Urns are also available in glass, metal, porcelain, marble or granite and they are labelled up with your loved one's name along with a certificate confirming details of the cremation.

You may decide to construct your own urn and include your own design as there is nothing to prevent you from doing so.

Wider choices for the disposal of cremated remains are available. These include placing a tiny amount of ashes into a glass paperweight, or having them inset into a piece of jewellery.

Top tip: It is possible to have a loved one cremated without the additional expense of a funeral director. Crematoria staff will help process the mandatory forms for you, and in some cases they will even keep the body refrigerated prior to the cremation, at a fraction of the cost of a funeral home. Also crematoria fees vary and are dependent on their refurbishment needs and general cash flow.

<u>Forms</u>

These forms are a legal requirement and are available from any crematorium. They are not just for the use of funeral directors. See the Forms section at the back of the book for more details.

- Application for cremation of the body or a person who has died
- Medical Certificate

Top tip: Ask your funeral director to choose a crematorium that is well-priced and within your budget. Prices vary considerably.

Chapter 7

Choosing a Cemetery or Catacomb

An Introduction to Cemeteries and Woodland Burials

A cemetery is defined as a burial ground. The Greek meaning for cemetery is: 'sleeping place', and it is within land that has been set aside for intact or cremated remains of deceased people to be interred. If the remains are to be interred into a grave it becomes a burial. If they are interred inside a grave that is above ground, such as a mausoleum or catacomb, it is referred to as a tomb.

Mutes and professional mourners were in great demand from the 1600s until the outbreak of the First World War in 1914, and were widely used in cemeteries throughout Europe. Mutes were always male and kept a vigil outside the door of the deceased's home and would later accompany the coffin to the cemetery for burial. Their appearance was often similar to that of the funeral director as they wore a traditional top hat with velvet ribbons attached. The exception was that mutes carried a heavy club, or wand concealed under a cape. Mutes were ceremonial protectors of the deceased, and by Victorian times their attendance at funerals was virtually mandatory because of the high demand for fresh bodies needed by physicians for medical research.

Charles Dickens' best-known mute was Oliver Twist. In the novel, the hen-pecked undertaker, Sowerberry, who specialised in children's funerals, employed him.

Professional mourners were usually women who would shriek and wail at funerals to encourage others to weep, and they are still in existence today in parts of Africa, the Philippines, and the Middle East.

Photo courtesy of Wrabness Woodland Burial Ground

Some woodland burial grounds, such as the one pictured above, allow families the opportunity of a single plot purchase with an optional tree planting service.

One of the key advantages of the Wrabness woodland burial ground, apart from its stunning location and close proximity to the river Stour, is that you are purchasing the grave as a freehold. This means that your family will never be asked for any additional funds in the future, unlike a traditional cemetery where the grave can be re-sold after the lease expires.

Woodland burial grounds offer idyllic locations for families wishing to conduct their own DIY funerals, thus potentially saving thousands of pounds on undertakers' fees.

The Woodland Burials group has three other idyllic sites located around the south of England. The first is at Oakfield Wood near Shamley Green in Surrey. Another is the Woodland of Remembrance which is situated just north of the village of Culford near Bury St Edmunds. And their Oakfield Wood site near Baughton can be found adjacent to the Severn Trent Water facility in Worcestershire.

There really is no fuss with a woodland burial and there is minimal paperwork to deal with. This means that any DIY funeral arrangement can be taken care of without worrying about unnecessary fees. In addition, families that follow a Muslim or Jewish faith have the freedom to bury their loved one's without delay, as is their custom.

Choosing a cemetery for a loved one is an important commitment. If your parish cemetery is full, it is worth asking the local authorities whether new land has recently been purchased. Another good idea would be to ask any stonemason, as they will be more than pleased to offer you some candid guidance. They are the professionals that have probably worked in numerous cemeteries or catacombs during their careers.

The Space Issue and Cemetery Fees

A lot of cemeteries often have a crematorium within their grounds. The demand for burial space has meant that many cemeteries have already been filled to capacity. Some cemeteries have purchased more land in order to increase their capacity for a few more years. But even they will inevitably reach full capacity one day.

It is a problem that councils and private landowners have wrestled with for years. Councillors are seriously considering supplying their cemeteries with vertical grave plots in an attempt to capitalise on as much space as possible.

Buyer beware:

Widower, Frank Blades, received an additional £160.00 bill to his wife's £6000.00 burial fee at Hannah Park Cemetery in Worksop Nottinghamshire because he stayed too long by her graveside at her funeral.

He was reportedly told by Hopkinsons funeral directors there was no rush to leave so he stayed for a while to pay his respects. He was later told by Hopkinsons that the council issue an additional fee when gravediggers are required to work beyond their contracted hours.

Fees

The fees involved in a cemetery funeral can be broken down as follows:

1. Plot Fees
2. Burial Fees

1. **Plot Fees**

   Plot fees are determined by the following factors:

   • A new grave purchase (which can be dug to allow a single burial, or up to four burials, or above in an existing grave with a raised lawn)
   • The re-opening of an existing grave
   • The interment of cremated remains

The cost of a new grave purchase depends on its location within the cemetery. Some graves carry a premium over others by virtue of their aesthetic positioning within the grounds. The trend now is to allow a family to choose and purchase a grave after the death has occurred because of the growing lack of available space. Also, the council responsible for the cemetery will automatically check postcodes and electoral roll entries to determine whether the grave purchased is for residents within the council's own district. If the cemetery of choice falls outside their postal area, the purchase fee is automatically doubled. So be certain that you (as next of kin) supply proof of residency, such as a utility bill or a listing on the electoral roll register.

2. **Burial Fees**

A standard burial fee applies to any cemetery for any deceased person that had been a bona fide resident that lived within the specified parish boundary postcode recognised by the local authority, for a new grave purchase. Even if your family has already purchased a family grave, there is an additional fee for the re-opening of an existing grave for burials of future family members.

Burial fees are usually doubled for families applying for the purchase of a new grave, living beyond a specified parish boundary, to ensure fairer availability for local residents.

Grave leases are variable depending on the cemetery, but normally vary between 75 and 100 years.

Woodland burials are beautiful and increasingly popular as people search for an idyllic resting place. Woodland burial grounds are divided up and priced according to their location and natural beauty within the burial site.

The basic fee structure for a woodland burial is very straightforward. Anyone can pre-purchase a plot in advance or at the time of need for an available grave. Different plots have different costs. Most plots are double (meaning that they are dug deep enough to house two coffins on top of each other). This means that you could bury another family member in the same spot at a later date. And, unlike a typical cemetery, there are no parish boundary surcharges applicable to people residing outside the borough.

Burial Fees for the Morbidly Obese

A new or existing grave that requires extra digging to accommodate oversize coffins for the morbidly obese automatically attract a double fee. This is because the overall capacity requires two grave spaces.

Forms

Application forms for a cemetery burial are available from most cemetery offices or the local authority that owns the cemetery.

Your application for burial forms should be returned to the bereavement office at your local district council, at least three days before the intended date of burial.

- When choosing a burial funeral make sure there is capacity for a new burial.
- Ask how much the grave fees are including the fee to re-open an existing grave before committing.
- Find out how much the cemetery fees are in case you need to employ a stonemason for renovation or cleaning work.
- Make sure the cemetery staff are specific about lease times because they vary.

Top tip: If you are the grave owner you are responsible for its upkeep. Why not visit the cemetery over a weekend and clean your loved one's headstone whilst the cemetery staff are at home. This will save an expensive cemetery fee.

How to clean your granite headstone:

Inspect the headstone for cracks and damage first.
If it is in good repair soak the headstone thoroughly first and use wooden scrapers or spatulas to remove any moss or growth from its surface and grooves first.
Mix one tablespoon of non-ionic soap with one gallon of water.
Use soft bristle brushes to apply the soapy mixture to the surface and scrub away any debris.
Keep the headstone wet at all times during the cleaning process working from the bottom up to prevent streaking.
Rinse the stone thoroughly with clean water.

How to clean your marble headstone:

Inspect the headstone for cracks and damage first.

Use plain hot water to wipe away any residue from the surface.
Work from the bottom upwards when cleaning.
Wipe the surface dry with a chamois but do not allow the stone to air dry.
Apply a marble polish to the surface and remember to follow the manufacturer's guidelines to restore a brilliant shine.

If cleaning is in advance of placing a memorial wreath, do not lay a wreath with a metal base because it will rust and stain.

Chapter 8

Choosing a Stonemason

An Introduction to Stonemasonry

The craft of the stonemason is rapidly evolving, and people often assume that booking a stonemason and a memorial headstone of your choice would all be a matter of course when a burial service is over.

Someone within your family may have used a stonemason many years ago and received an excellent service with value for money. But when the time comes to re-book the same company again there will be many new regulations and inter-company policies to deal with.

In 2004, the British Register of Accredited Memorial Masons (BRAMM) scheme was set up with the aim of establishing a network of nationally accredited businesses and registered fixers that would ultimately have individual registration schemes. The aims were mainly to maintain high standards, recognise health and safety aspects, and promote closer working relationships between memorial masons and the burial authorities.

For the many long-established stonemasons this was a regulation that went too far, and was just another unnecessary expense. A listing on the BRAMM register requires meeting strict criteria. Many stonemasons are successful, and many more are not. Every church falls within a district borough council, and each borough has its own set of rules and regulations regarding the shape and style of headstones. Even the allowable sizes of the stonework will vary. Cemeteries operate different sets of fees throughout the boroughs.

How to Choose a Stonemason

Cemetery offices have their own lists of approved or recognised stonemasons, and it is worth beginning your enquiries at the cemetery office.

When There is a Monopoly

It might come as a big surprise to discover that your friendly, local stonemason whom you have known and entrusted previously is no longer permitted to enter your chosen crematorium garden or cemetery, even with a BRAMM (British Register of Accredited Memorial Masons) certificate.

You may find you have no choice other than to use the only approved stonemason recognised by the cemetery for their district. It is logical that you will end up paying far more than intended. It is fair to assume that competitor stonemasons could reasonably take the cemetery to court and force them to issue entry permits. But by doing so the local authority or cemetery in question might combat the challenge by making their permit fees astronomical.

Quotes

Stonemasons tend to base their prices on the elements involved with each job. Supplying a vase or adding a new inscription to an existing headstone is often not worth their while. Instead, they prefer to specialise in the supply of quality headstones, which are sourced at the lowest price, and then retailed for as much as possible.

Top tip: You have nothing to lose by negotiating and driving some very hard bargains.

Materials & Costs

- Marble. The appearance and longevity of a headstone depends on the material it is made from. Marble is exceptionally beautiful and easy to cut (and it is also much cheaper to purchase than granite). Unfortunately, it is highly porous and can deteriorate rapidly once permanently exposed to the elements. Its best usage is within the interior design and structure of a church or cathedral where it can be appreciated for its beauty over the centuries.

- Granite. Granite headstones last virtually forever, provided nobody reverses a vehicle into them or they become vandalised. The top end of the world granite market for figurines and headstones originate from China. This premium black granite is known as 'Shanxi black' throughout the trade. Most medium-sized and reputable stonemasons purchase as much as 40 tonnes of this high quality stone every year. Stonemasons striving to maximise profits often source cheaper and inferior grades of black granite from other parts of Asia. When fixed, installed and inscribed, most people would be unable to differentiate between Shanxi and Asian granite. The test of quality becomes apparent when inferior stonework suddenly loses its sheen. It is also worth bearing in mind that headstones lean over a period of time due to soil subsidence.

Designs & Costs

- Emblems. Any emblem drawn onto a headstone should be intricate, resemble its intended design and remain aesthetically-appealing for generations to come. However, if the stonemason relies purely on the guidance of a cheap stencil when producing an emblem that should be everlasting, they will eventually encounter problems. To draw a quality flower by hand for instance is much more labour-intensive but has far greater definition than a stencil could possibly achieve, but he will charge you much more for this.

- Headstone etchings. Personalised images taken from photographs can be recreated with startling realism. Laser etchings have the best effect on black or on dark grey granite because they create a sharp, light grey impression. This form of artwork is becoming increasingly popular and is proving to be an excellent way of recreating your loved one's image from a cherished photograph. Other popular choices are etchings of a special pet or landscape scene. These can be customised according to your budget.

Top tip: Paying more will save you money in the long term if everlasting quality, craftsmanship and a superior design are what you are looking for.

Guaranteed Workmanship

It should be possible for a stonemason to offer a virtual lifelong guarantee and therefore it follows that all etchings and inscriptions should also last forever. Placing a wreath or object on a marble headstone at Christmas, for instance, could become a costly exercise because it will stain – and when the stonemason is ultimately blamed he will insist that any cleaning bill is paid by you, the grave owner. A stonemason could be liable for any stonework they supplied and fixed for up to 19 years. They may be asked to carry out unplanned maintenance work, adjust, or clean headstones recorded to them. It is a far more practical solution for stonemasons to help their clients choose granite memorials instead of marble.

Chapter 9
Choosing a Florist

Floral images courtesy of: Funeral Flowers Network

An Introduction to Funeral Floristry

Funeral flowers reflect the depth of love and feelings that people have for whomever has passed away. The occupation or character of the deceased can be recreated and reflected in the style of the floral tribute. For instance, a songwriter or musician might have a floral frame with musical notes depicted. A competent florist can recreate virtually anything, in any size, and once commissioned it is their responsibility to deliver their completed work of art to the funeral home, intact and on time.

Some tributes are more intricate and complex than others, but all are labour-intensive. Every florist works to a deadline, and they will hardly ever say no to an order. Their overheads in relation to any profit margins are by and large very high. Therefore, the chances of a florist refusing your order are minimal.

Whenever someone passed away in years gone by it became a tradition to shower the funeral parlour with a sea of flowers on the morning of the funeral. Every car connected to the funeral would be laden with an array of flowers attached carefully to the chrome bars on the roof of its limousines and hearse. But with spiralling funeral costs year on year, the expense of large floral arrangements has become too great for most families. The customary norm these days is for families to suggest that their mourners offer a charitable donation as an alternative to spending money on flowers.

Nevertheless, a lot of people still prefer to take a tribute of flowers so they can attach a personal message of condolence. Whenever an elderly patient has received palliative care over a long period, friendships develop between the nursing staff and the patient. Their friendship extends through to the patient's entire family and those affections are represented through flowers at the funeral.

Florists set off for the flower markets in their vans, often covering long distances in the early hours, to source freshly-cut flowers and special oasis templates for their orders. When they return, their work is gruelling and often interrupted by telephone enquiries and many things that can go wrong. Your tribute could potentially appear tired, battered, or past its best, by the time it arrives at its destination. Any florist will endeavour to prevent mistakes from happening and loathe poor workmanship, but they are all human and are often asked to perform superhuman tasks within incredibly tight deadlines.

How to Choose a Florist

Funeral flowers vary in price and floral designers can be expensive, but they are artists in their right. Most good florists tend to be recommended by local funeral directors or they may be linked to Interflora.

- Study your local florists' websites and how they present themselves. Read their testimonials and reviews.
- Which florists do your local funeral homes recommend?
- Visit their branch. Are they friendly, approachable, busy, and well-presented?
- Ascertain who their commercial clients are: hotels, business premises?
- Check whether they have won any business awards.
- Look at their work portfolio to discover their creativity.
- Can they work within a set budget?

How to Choose a Floral Arrangement

Florists keep a brochure or photo albums of floral ideas, which are priced accordingly. Ordering floral letters, spelling out someone's name in full, or using a family member's title can be expensive, and are priced per letter.

Top tip: GRANDMA retails cheaper as NAN; BENJAMIN retails cheaper as BEN.

The prices that florists charge varies between geographical areas and from shop to shop, in the same way that the cost of funerals varies around the country. Lilies make a delightful floral tribute, but are probably the most expensive flower to purchase from a florist.

There will nearly always be some scope for negotiation at a florist depending on the time of year and how much notice they are given to complete a more complex floral arrangement.

If a funeral happens to coincide with February 14th, the likelihood of getting a discount will be remote because the florist will be working around the clock to be certain that their orders are delivered in time for Valentine's Day. Also, the normally high standards of care and attention to detail may suffer due to their already excessive workload.

Top tip: Many people are unaware of how long floral tributes are left on display at a crematorium and the policy varies around the country. It is worth checking, particularly during busy periods, to save disappointment.

Funeral Flowers Network are the UK's only flower relay company specifically for the funeral industry. The company works alongside the NFFD (The National Federation of Funeral Directors) and all flowers are provided by approved members of the NFFD.

Floral images courtesy of: Funeral Flowers Network

Chapter 10

Choosing a Minister or Celebrant

What Do Ministers Do?

To become an ordained minister is certainly no easy career journey for anyone to suddenly embark upon. Ideally, the applicant would be young, from a Christian family and have been to a church school. As the privileges of such a childhood are too elusive for many, then Sunday school, along with a regular local church attendance, would definitely help. Prospective ministers should, at least, gain a thorough knowledge and understanding of the Holy Bible, including the Old and New Testaments. They should also have some empathy and compassion for people and, of course, a genuine liking of them. By nature they will possess a gregarious flare and shrug off any feelings of shyness or introversion. Nothing should be allowed to impede the character of a minister. After all, their job is to be a pillar of society (except when they fall foul of the law and decimate an entire banking group as the former ex-Methodist Minister and Co-operative Banking Group Executive, Paul Flowers, achieved so recklessly).

It may seem surprising that a natural ability to sing is not their pre-requisite qualification. They speak with clarity and seasoned authority. But having captivated their congregation with such mesmerising finesse, it is then completely irksome for everyone to witness their appalling hymn recitals where singing is, at best, flat and off-key. A pre-recorded choral version, or a professional artist's recording, works every time and does not attract ridicule.

Suggestion to all Ministers: Why not, for the sake of your mourners, step away from the microphones? Perhaps even sit down and do not attempt to sing unless you have had plenty of singing lessons.

Okay, they are not all that bad. But the good ones are few and far between.

The funeral services they deliver are almost a 'one size fits all' template of prayers, blessings, hymns and psalms that contain a standard format suitable for any family. Only the name of the deceased is changed within an over-regurgitated script for the benefit of the mourners. Ministers have their own style of delivery and personality. Some are able to produce the most professional of services, in the same way they would conduct a christening or a wedding. Sadly, others do not, and when the minister's ramblings are too short, or if the deceased is wrongly named, letters of complaint are bound to follow. It becomes the discretion of the funeral director to honour a discount for mistakes made during the service by a member of the clergy. Negotiation should achieve an all-round satisfactory outcome, particularly if a minister is prepared to waive their fee. Just like every other aspect of funeral arranging, minister's fees go up every year and vary across the parishes. As a rule of thumb, their fee for taking a funeral service should not exceed £200 (prices correct as of 2015).

How to Choose a Minister

Your funeral arranger will have a list of ministers to contact for your loved one's service and will invariably choose one of their personal favourites, without any particular reference to you.

You will be asked if you prefer the service to be religious or non-religious. If you had previously attended a local funeral and were impressed with the minister throughout the service, describe who he or she was and ask your arranger to check their availability. If you do not express a preference, the outcome of who is chosen to officiate the funeral service could end up being something of a lottery.

On one hand, a good minister will make an appointment with you, and work out various aspects of the service with your entire family present during a pleasant and professional meeting. And so they should too, as each family has the right to know exactly whom their arranger has entrusted to officiate their loved one's funeral.

On the other hand, the minister may only telephone you a day or two in advance of the funeral and take basic instructions over the phone.

Whenever possible, your funeral arranger will try and get as much information from you, the client, during your visit. Your choice of music will be discussed along with any requests for hymns, choir or desire for an organist. If the choices are known, they will be ordered in advance of the funeral through a company specialising in supplying music at funeral services.

There are occasions when a minister categorically refuses to officiate a service if a request has been made containing a variety of chart songs with no allowance for hymns. For the deeply pious, only 'proper' hymns and psalms are acceptable. One of the most common examples of 'unacceptability', in the eyes of the more stoic, clergy members, is the classic *Monty Python* track: *Always*

Look on the Bright Side. This song has now become popular at funerals as the ideal track for 'music for reflection', and there is even a clean version available for families that do not want to hear a particular swear word.

This is one extreme example, but what is wrong with requesting John Lennon's beautiful song *Imagine*? Most people find the lyrics of the track extremely moving. Until you consider it from a minister's perspective:

"Imagine no heaven. It's easy if you try; below us no hell, above us only sky."

You might think, "So what?" But for many ministers these lyrics are simply too hard to swallow and downright offensive, particularly as the lyrics suddenly bring the entire purpose of religion into question:

"... nothing to kill or die for, and no religion too..."

Other examples of songs that are unacceptable to members of the clergy include:

> *Highway to Hell*, by AC/DC
> *You'll Never Get to Heaven*, by Diana Vickers
> *Buried Alive*, by Avenged Sevenfold

These days, a 'celebration of life' style of funeral service is growing in popularity as people try and give their loved ones a special send-off, because they are much more relaxed and personalised. So if a college student's favourite track had been *Highway to Hell*, why should it not be one of the song choices at the funeral?

It could be argued that within the privacy of a chapel the family should have the right to organise their loved one's funeral service in any way that is befitting to the deceased, regardless of anybody else's point of view.

What Do Celebrants Do?

Celebrants focus on 'the celebration' of a person's life where the focus is about what someone did and their personality characteristics. They tend to be dedicated, broad-minded and worldly individuals. They are happy to work closely with families before officiating a semi-religious or non-religious funeral. Their ethos towards officiating a funeral is pretty much "a celebration of life" and that they are performing "the final event of someone's life". It is all about having the ability to provide each family with as many elements as possible (and not necessarily what the clergy would prefer) to reflect, honour and respect whomever had passed away. They are professional wordsmiths with an ability to create factual and imaginative eulogies. The impact that a celebrant (or minister) makes throughout the service will help a family find closure.

Most celebrants charge roughly the same fee as a clergy minister, but the family is more likely to receive greater attention, including a more detailed, accurate and personalised eulogy script. Firstly, the celebrant will arrange a personal visit to meet the family prior to the funeral. They will ask everything about the deceased's entire life and then set about writing a script with anecdotes, tributes and poems. If your wish is to add a prayer or hymn into the service because of the potential amount of people that are likely to attend, the celebrant is flexible enough to make it possible. Some mourners may find it offensive, for example, not to hear *The Lord's Prayer*.

Fees become extremely expensive whenever a Humanist is requested (by at least double in some cases). Their roles are often confused with those of a celebrant, and celebrants are often mistakenly referred to as Humanists.

Definition of a Humanist: an individual with a rationalised outlook or system of thought, attaching prime importance to human rather than divine or supernatural matters.

Definition of a celebrant: an individual who specialises in the celebration of someone's life through the spoken word at a funeral, a wedding, a baby naming ceremony or any other event requiring a ceremony.

The work of a funeral celebrant has to be a prosaic review, regardless of any mistakes and wrong paths that the deceased may have taken through life, which are then subtly watered down with the use of more gentle portrayals. For instance, an unpleasant episode involving an acrimonious divorce could be simplified to, "and when life eventually came between them, Jack and Linda simply went their separate ways". Some religious ministers are good at this, whilst others are not, and when the ministers' focus lies clearly with a structured Biblical purpose, then he is likely to spend less time describing the deceased. This is worth thinking about if you want a very personal service.

Many mid-management employees (especially teaching and nursing professionals) choose alternative ways of making a living by hoping to become celebrants. On the face of it, being good with people and having an ability to write descriptively seems an appropriate career transition. But why are so few able to make a sustainable living, when it is potentially theirs to have?

A celebrant who is new to the circuit will, of course, be presentable, well-spoken, learned in the ways of clever prose and the spoken word, knowledgeable about funeral protocol, forever punctual, willing to meet clients, always in the very best frame of mind and generally tick all the boxes that will be required of them.

But there will be two critical 'tick box' tests for them to overcome.

Test 1: When the funeral service is over, the arranger will receive some general feedback from the conductor who was present during the funeral. Feedback will include the celebrant's overall style, conduct and performance.

Test 2: A day or two after the service, the arranger will try and ascertain from the family how things went generally throughout the service and how happy they were with the performance of the celebrant.

This process will be ongoing throughout the celebrant's career and they will soon learn that it is just as crucial to look after the needs of the arranger, as those of the family. But even with the very best experience, those 'dry spells' can occur for no apparent reason when their bookings dry up. This happens even when everything has gone well and each family had expressed a total satisfaction with the celebrant. The business is highly competitive and funeral homes always keep a long list of celebrants' names on their books.

A celebrant should remain calm and in control even when a funeral director arrives late or has forgotten to bring a personal effect that has been written into the script. Funeral directors make mistakes and things can, and often do, go badly wrong.

This is true of celebrants too. A single word spoken in error has the potential to turn a funeral arranger cold forever and destroy their entire business. For a celebrant to deliver a well-constructed and impactive eulogy within a 25 minute time slot, an average of 1,800 words will need to be written with skill and flare.

Too few words and the service will finish uncomfortably fast. Too many and the service is in danger of over-running. For a service to run smoothly, to time and efficiently, takes a considerable amount of skill. The policy of some crematoria is to fine any funeral director responsible for allowing their service booking to overrun.

But sooner or later, the professional celebrant, or minister will inevitably pick up one or two black marks relating to their performance or professionalism. Examples include: referring to people incorrectly, e.g. Bill instead of Billy; not sitting down during a piece of music; looking at the ceiling for too long; appearing too jolly or too miserable; whether the conductor likes him/her or not; leaving it too long to return a call when being offered a booking.

The list is endless and on the face of it trivial, but for the majority of arrangers the celebrant has now complicated the entire funeral and will therefore not be rebooked. It is not unknown for ministers who could be 'led into temptation' by creating rumours about other ministers or celebrants. This occurs when an established minister feels vulnerable because other people are receiving too many bookings.

There are surprisingly few funeral arrangers with sufficient knowledge or expertise to construct a funeral eulogy, let alone have the confidence to speak in public. Nevertheless, they cultivate a common perception that celebrants receive too much money for their 25 minutes of work.

How to Choose a Celebrant

Even the most established celebrants are faced with colossal competition. Any celebrant worth his salt will have their own website explaining their experience and how they are different from the rest. Testimonials that are highlighted within their websites can sometimes be verified by a number of local funeral arrangers and funeral directors.

Most funeral homes will tell you whom their preferred or regular celebrants are, and will be happy to advise you; although it does not always follow that their opinion is the correct one.

Top tips:

- *Many funeral arrangers assume that their say is final when it comes to booking the type of minister for a funeral service, as well as whom should receive the service booking (and whom should not). It does not take much for a minister to become an arranger's favourite individual one month, only to be ignored the next. You are not obliged to follow the arranger's choice of minister if you already have an individual in mind.*
- *Fees vary between humanists, members of the clergy and professional celebrants. Make sure your arranger understands the differences between these groups and knows how much they charge to conduct a service.*
- *Alternatively, conduct your own service for free if your family feels capable of doing so.*

Chapter 11

Choosing an Appropriate Coffin or Casket

Photo courtesy of Bellacouche

Every funeral home has a selection of glossy coffin brochures close to hand for you to browse through. A coffin is potentially the most expensive box frame you will ever purchase. They are a necessary purchase and funeral directors know their coffins will be chosen directly from a photograph within a matter of seconds.

A coffin, in basic terms, is a six to eight-sided funerary box with a lid and a base, and is used for the containment of a dead person, which is later displayed to mourners for a short time. In America the box is called a casket and has four sides, with a lid and a base.

Standard coffins are bought in bulk and are stored upright at a funeral home. They come in a vast range of imperial sizes such as, 5' 8" x 18", 6' 2" x 22" and so on. For the unfortunate families with loved ones that were profoundly obese at death, a custom-made coffin will be required. They are constructed at up to a staggering 8' x 4' and require a double burial plot purchase because of their dimensions. As customised coffins are designed to contain bodies weighing up to 70 stone (nearly half a ton), specialist equipment will also be needed when lowering into the grave.

Types of Coffins

It is an integral part of any funeral director's business to offer a catalogue of coffins in different styles, shapes, colours and materials. The printing of coffin brochures is costly and they are often in short supply in funeral homes. You should request a brochure, but if they cannot supply one then rest assured that your final coffin choice will have been influenced by whomever you discussed the funeral arrangements with.

The materials used for coffin construction around the world vary from steel, an assortment of wooden frames, recycled cardboard, banana leaves and even fibreglass. However, realistically the final decision for an appropriate shape, style and suitability of the coffin material lies with each crematorium, or Parish Council.

1. Basic coffin

Basic coffins a re ideal for a cremation funeral because it will be destroyed in the cremator along with the deceased.

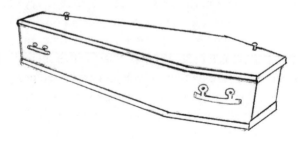

2. Basic casket

Basic caskets are ideal for a cremation funeral or an earth burial. They are designed for either purpose.

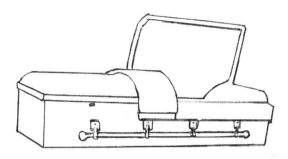

3. Coloured coffin

The designs printed on a coloured coffin are as simple, or complex, as required depending on your budget

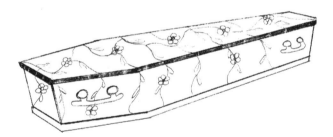

4. Wicker coffin

Wicker coffins can be constructed in many designs.

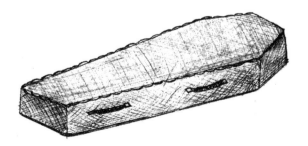

5. Cardboard coffin

When a family requests "simplicity", a cardboard coffin is certainly the answer. They are extremely sturdy, bio-degradable and ideal for a woodland or earth burial.

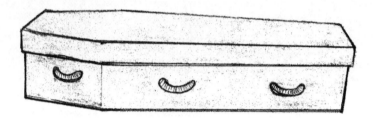

6. Typical Ghanaian coffin depicting whatever someone did during their life

The visual impact of a personalised construction of an achievement in life is always impressive.

7. Bamboo coffins

The designs for a bamboo coffin are numerous and can be less expensive than a wooden coffin. Bamboo is 100% bio-degradable.

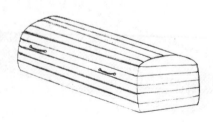

In England, any coffin interred above ground must be sealed by law. This requires having a lead liner within the coffin shell.

Top tips:

- *When arranging a cremation service, a basic coffin will suffice because it is only on display for a short time and will be destroyed after the service.*
- *You could construct your own coffin using the approved materials, or purchase one from a funeral director that is compassionate enough to sell a coffin without a complete funeral package.*

Members of the public are now able to approach the industry directly through a new division of the NFFD (National Federation of Funeral Directors) known as Funeralstore: www.funeralstore.co.uk

As well as supplying funeral homes, the company boasts a wide selection of coffins for anyone to purchase at the cheapest possible price. For instance, they sell a wicker coffin for several hundred pounds cheaper than their competitors:

You may also like to have a look at: www.comparethecoffin. com

Retail costs rise every year and an early purchase will definitely save money.

- A basic coffin looks fine and is ample for a cremation funeral as it will be destroyed.
- If you prefer a more elaborate coffin, such as, a coloured coffin; wicker; a higher- graded wooden coffin or casket, expect the purchase price to be significantly higher.
- Consider contacting the Funeralstore before trying to construct your own coffin.

Chapter 12
Choosing a Mode of Transport

Photo courtesy of: A Wakelin

Photo courtesy of:
Motorcycle Funerals Ltd

WHEELS Midland Red
Collection
Photo courtesy of:
Drayhorse Shires

A burial at sea
Photo courtesy of:
The Britannia Shipping
Company

Most funeral directors operate using a fleet of black vehicles consisting of one or two hearses and several limousines. The traditional colour of black has prevailed since Queen Victoria's mourning for her beloved Prince Albert in 1861. Her grief was completely overwhelming and lasted 40 years until her own death in 1901. During those four decades, Queen Victoria invariably wore black, which became the symbolic colour of the day. It was worn by anyone with an allegiance to the Sovereign and was therefore followed by virtually everyone. Even the Royal Park had its gates painted black by order, as did so many other public places.

The legacy from this solemn historical period continues within the British psyche today, including funerals and funeral directors. Young people tend to dress in a sober black attire, perhaps in a subliminal attempt to conform to a safe traditional dress code that lost its original meaning and purpose more than a century ago. Even so, they all admire their fashionable European neighbours who experiment comfortably with more relaxed and vibrant colours, making them appear less bothered about formal fashion regulations.

The majority of funeral directors are also reluctant to break away from their traditional image for fear of losing their century-old identity, or 'mark of respect'. But there are plenty of interesting alternatives if you are prepared to shop around. Some funeral directors in recent years have opted for a two-tone style image to colour their funeral vehicles, mixing silver with black, and even presenting their entire fleet in silver.

European hearses are based on commercial vans, and in the past, small vans could easily be converted into hearses. These days, Mercedes-Benz vans are common within most fleets. Independent funeral directors use luxurious brands of cars for image and the majority are Mercedes-Benz, Rolls Royce, Daimler, Jaguar, Volvo and Vauxhall. Co-operative Funeralcare operates a fleet of Coleman Milne vehicles that were designed and manufactured for the funeral market. Dignity use Mercedes vehicles as well as a variety of vehicles that appear slightly different in design.

It became fashionable through the Breast Cancer Awareness campaigns during the 1990s to wear a small pink ribbon or badge on a jacket lapel. When a death occurs as a result of this dreadful disease, it is now possible to hire funeral vehicles that are totally pink. This helps punctuate the importance of the cancer awareness campaign and the devastating impact that the disease has on families.

The Cortege

Have you ever observed a funeral cortege passing by and wondered why its vehicles are driven so tightly together?

In most small towns and rural locations, pedestrians and drivers alike slow down out of courtesy for the family and the deceased, wherever the cortege happens to be at that moment. They are genuinely proud to show their respect and concern for a family's sad loss and the cortege travels on without interruption or incident. Cities, on the other hand, are packed with busy people who have no patience for the living, let alone the dead. For people with hectic lifestyles, the sight of a funeral cortege is no less annoying than a slow-moving articulated lorry. Intrusions such as these bring out the worst in human nature and people sometimes think nothing of overtaking, or seizing an opportunity to cut in if they are able to get away with it. Such foolhardy actions are bound to aggravate a conductor or the drivers as they attempt to protect the cortege.

1. Seating

The seating protocol during a funeral cortege suggests that immediate family members travel together in the first limousine. Each limousine accommodates six mourners and the conductor travels in the front passenger seat of car one. If additional limousines are required for other relatives, such as cousins or step children, they will travel in car two, car three, and so on. When a conductor, or funeral director, gets the seating arrangements wrong it causes tension and annoyance within the family. Families tend to be very supportive of each other at funerals and the death of a family member usually unites everyone.

Sometimes the seating arrangements are purposely jumbled up when a funeral director suspects divisions and hostilities among family members that are likely to turn violent because of the heightened emotions that a funeral can create. This can and does happen where jealousies occur between siblings and their partners, or ex-partners. Funerals have the potential to tear families apart. But planning funeral arrangements properly in advance helps diffuse many of the unnecessary tensions (refer to Chapter 24: Pre-paid Funeral Planning).

2. **Horses**

Funeral horses and their carriages are either black or white, and their breeds are chosen for their strength and ability to cope in traffic conditions. The black Friesian breed are powerful and majestic, and the slightly smaller, white Hungarian breed are just as capable of transporting your loved one to a dignified funeral. A traditional black hearse carriage, pulled by a pair of black Friesians, is normally a cheaper option of than white carriages pulled by a pair of white Hungarians.

The labour involved in stabling horses; maintaining expensive funeral carriages and keeping them in pristine condition, along with countless hours of polishing tack for each horse team, requires unlimited commitment, a lot of space, and a supply of specialist grooms.

Very few funeral directors own sufficient land for the organisation of any stabling and livery facility. Instead they simply hire them in for any funerals requiring horse-drawn carriages. The horse-drawn carriage hire charges are huge for any funeral director that does not manage its own stables.

Top tips:

- *You could do the same. Most funeral directors will add a mark-up of at least 30% for arranging this service. Contact your local livery and see if you can book the horses directly.*
- *Funeral horses usually travel up to a maximum of seven miles (approximately). If your destination is greater than seven miles and a second team of horses is required, you can negotiate an excellent price that would normally be granted to the funeral director.*

3. **Motorbikes**

To give a motorcycle enthusiast the perfect send-off, it is possible to arrange for a motorbike (usually a Harley Davidson or Triumph) with a base welded to its side to accommodate a loved one's coffin. The death of a motorcycle enthusiast tends to draw a large attendance at a funeral, and the distinctive growl of a Harley Davidson leading the way to a chapel is a very poignant and powerful statement.

Funeral directors will hire the services of a fully-trained motorcycle professional that will deliver the coffin punctually, and with all the razzmatazz and power expected at a biker's funeral.

Top tip: Source your own motorbike funeral company and deal with them direct. Otherwise the funeral director will make a similar phone call and add their mark-up in the same way they would for a horse-drawn funeral.

4. __At Sea__

Burials at sea are not restricted to people that had once served at sea with the Royal Navy. Anyone with a particular interest in a burial at sea can use either the services of a specialist funeral director, or have one arranged through the Royal Navy, depending on their budget. An enquiry made directly to a specialist burial at sea company would be cheaper than going through a funeral director.

- There are a lot of innovative ways of transporting your loved one to a funeral these days. It is a highly competitive market where deals can be made.

Chapter 13

Embalming. Is it Really Necessary?

An Introduction to Embalming

When a person dies, a series of chemical and biologically-destructive processes become triggered. The process begins slowly at first, depending on: the cause of death; when the death occurred and the age; or condition of the deceased at the time of death. These are only primary factors, but there are several others that also apply.

The average human body contains approximately 100 trillion cells, which are programmed to self-destruct when death has occurred. Funeral directors face a bit of a problem when it comes to explaining to families what happens during the embalming process. They cleverly fudge over the issue as quickly as possible, using every euphemism known, such as "hygienic treatment" and "caring for your loved one". This is because embalming is intrusive, brutal and quite nauseating for the uninitiated. Fortunately for the majority of families they have absolutely no idea what any of it entails and agree to it within the overall blur of the funeral package.

The first logical reason for embalming a body is to saturate and sanitise all the cell tissues using specialist chemicals through arterial injection, rendering all waterborne and airborne pathogens as harmless. Otherwise, the funeral staff and anyone else in contact with the body, along with anyone else those people may have come into contact with, are all potentially at risk from infection.

Funeral homes that tend not to embalm, unless they really have to (in order to save money), may be taking foolhardy risks.

The second reason for embalming is to preserve a body long enough for a viewing to take place before the funeral. Embalming will only halt the process of decomposition for the short term.

The third reason is for presentation. The purpose of presenting a deceased person to their loved ones is to make them appear at rest and at peace. The image of what their loved ones are shown will stay with them for the rest of their lives and embalmers will always endeavour to do their best. But in reality, things do not always go according to plan.

Imagine that you own a beautiful Ming vase and that it is decorated with the finest, delicate artwork and intricate detail for everyone to admire. Then one day, it gets knocked over and breaks into a thousand pieces. A skilled craftsman could carefully glue it all back together again, piece by piece, returning your treasured vase in one piece. Your friends will still admire it, despite any inevitable blemishes, but you will always be aware that it will never quite look the same again. In a way, embalming a body is no different from the analogy of repairing the Ming vase. Some people argue that the outcome is similar but rarely exact because the personality of the deceased no longer exists.

The embalmer acts as the unseen broker between the funeral director and the family. The craft of an embalmer solidifies a family's trust in having chosen the funeral director to look after their loved ones. Embalmers have to prioritise which of the deceased's cases to prepare first, depending on the date of the funeral and when family members are likely to view.

When a body has become too badly decomposed or has been horrifically mutilated, it is the responsibility of the embalmer, including the funeral director, not to allow anyone to view. In extreme situations, when people have been involved in multiple trauma incidents, such as a major traffic incidents, fires, or rail disasters, some families still insist that they pay their last respects by viewing their loved ones before the funeral. Embalmers are highly-trained specialists that have to deal with every type of incident.

But a body that has been so badly wounded or scarred requires specialist embalming, which takes more time, additional materials and chemicals, cosmetics and a great deal of skill. There are several embalmers who specialise in this area and their professionalism is reflected in their fees.

But is it really worth it? When a body has been so badly mutilated that it contains more visible plaster of Paris than human tissue, why pay thousands of pounds for an almost fake image that is potentially too disturbing to see anyway?

Embalming is anatomical; biological; mathematical; chemical; physiological, as well as psychological. There is a lot to get right and many funeral directors decide not to get involved with things they do not fully understand, are too complex or possibly controversial. Therefore, their policy is not to offer any embalming or family viewing service at all. However, others are much more opportunistic and mark up everything to make a profit.

Training to be an embalmer is seriously hard work, and The British Institute of Embalming has set a benchmark for a minimum 60% mark in order to pass each of its six modules. Then, a practical examination involving a 'straight case', followed by a 'post mortem case' will prove the student's total understanding of embalming science and an adequate level of dexterity within a mortuary environment. Finally, after spending a small fortune and a couple of intense study years, the student is at last officially BIE-qualified. Then they are able to promote themselves as trade embalmers.

But the reality of working all hours in a cold, busy mortuary seems a world away from the textbook and laborious classroom practical techniques of embalming. The mortuary of the real world is completely void of mathematical equations, such as:

IQ = CV (index of concentrated fluid x quantity of concentrated fluid = strength of diluted fluid x volume of diluted fluid)

Forget it Gunga Din! From here on in, everything works commercially:

Experience x speed = efficiency x possible outcomes x income

In other words, 'smoke and mirrors' wherever necessary will help keep a funeral director happy, including the families of the deceased.

And as for the hard-earned embalming qualification? As yet it is not even a legal requirement and theoretically anyone with some anatomical knowledge (and a strong stomach) can legally perform an embalming operation. When embalmers work their daily craft they are only applying about 20% of the coursework that they had laboured intensely over throughout their embalming training.

Trade embalmers prefer to intubate arteries that are quick to locate, such as the brachial artery instead of the textbook left and right carotid arteries located in the neck, as practiced for their BIE coursework. Time will always be of the essence in a mortuary.

What Happens if the Job is Done Badly?

When post-embalming purges occur, a body may purge in two ways:

1. A lung purge emits a pinkish fluid from the nose
2. A stomach purge emits a brown fluid from the mouth

If any visual purging occurs, it is classed as a bad outcome and the embalmer (assuming there is one) has worked carelessly.

What If The Funeral Home Doesn't Embalm The Body?

Buyer beware: There are some funeral directors that do not believe in embalming at all, and others who employ unqualified (or inexperienced) members of staff, which could impact on the quality of the embalming operation. If you have a bad experience when paying your last respects, demand a substantial reduction from your funeral bill.

Some funeral directors refuse to accept any necessity to embalm bodies and suffice with applying a basic septum suture, or a round mandibular mouth suture. This procedure is also known as 'setting the features', which creates the expression, and in some cases, prevents residual purging. It also saves the funeral home time and money, but attracts criticism among other funeral directors who provide a full embalming service.

Top tips:
- *Write a letter of consent to a medical school donating your body for medical science. If your body is donated to a medical school for anatomical research, or for educational and testing purposes, the medical school will cremate your body for nothing once they have finished studying it.*

- *If hygienic treatment, aka embalming, is not required, make sure that your funeral director has not included it within your final funeral bill.*
- *If your funeral director invites you to see your loved one in a chapel of rest prior to the funeral, you may have grounds for a discount if embalming standards are poor.*

Chapter 14

The Chapel of Rest – to View or Not to View

"Well, she's not pretty and she's not awful.
She's just... pretty awful."

Every funeral home has at least one chapel of rest where families are able to pay their last respects in the privacy of a quiet, peaceful room. The tranquil, special atmosphere is contained within windowless surroundings and varies greatly from funeral home to funeral home. A lot depends on the imagination of the funeral director and how they think a chapel of rest should appear, as well as their budget. A heavy velvet curtain is usually draped across a locked door at the end of the room that leads directly to the mortuary area behind it.

The loss of a relative, friend or partner is an extremely sad and emotional time for anyone, even when death had been expected. Most people choose to visit their loved ones again before the day of the funeral to provide comfort and offer a form of closure, which is all part of the grieving process. Time spent alone with a loved one in a chapel of rest is a private moment.

Families that choose not to visit their loved ones have their own personal and valid reasons. It could be that they are quite simply too fearful, inappropriately young, or extremely sensitive. It all becomes a matter of personal choice. Some religions state that a body must be buried within 24 hours of death, and it is assumed the soul of the deceased will remain tormented up to the moment the body is laid to rest.

Only the bereaved can decide whether or not to proceed with visiting a chapel of rest. Nevertheless, they need to be made aware that once the door to the chapel has opened, their loved one, whom they have known and cherished over the years, will be lying in a coffin supported by a pair of wooden trestles – all within an environment that you may find very strange.

The body has to be washed, embalmed and dressed prior to your arrival to minimise any risk of infection to you. Most embalmers do a remarkable job at making people appear better in death than they appeared during the final stages of life. The embalmer's skills come to the fore as they make the deceased appear comfortable and at rest.

A funeral director will inform the next of kin whenever viewing a loved one is inappropriate. For instance, when deep scarring occurs after a major incident, or when a body is in a bad state of decomposition and viewing becomes unhygienic, or too traumatic.

Many larger funeral companies have adapted several chapels of rest to cater for greater quantities of families, particularly during busy periods when the death rate is at its highest throughout the colder winter months. Mortuaries are designed to hold dozens of deceased people along with their coffins. Their loved ones can view them privately, often more than once. But when the pressure is on and the staff are at their busiest, an overstretched receptionist might accidentally allow a family to enter a chapel for viewing – and present them with the wrong body. After all, there are many people who share the same surname in this world and mistakes happen. Some families are much more forgiving than others, and the boxes of tissues are not just used by grieving relatives.

Top tip: If you have decided that viewing your loved one in a chapel of rest is not for you, tell the funeral director not to charge you for something you do not require.

Hopefully, the American practice of charging a family an additional viewing fee has not become too widespread. It's new and Co-operative Funeralcare are also considering it, so buyer beware.

Chapter 15

Planning a Wake

People who pass through the gates of a crematorium or cemetery do so to pay their respects and offer support to a family. They may not have been to a crematorium before, and will have no idea where they are going or what to expect during the service, and as they make their way slowly down the driveway they may experience a whole range of emotions. The event becomes increasingly surreal and a variety of abnormal emotions are suddenly in force as people enter a grief-stricken environment.

As the allocated time for the service approaches, more people are likely to arrive and the waiting room will begin to fill with a mixture of familiar and unfamiliar faces. Families become separated and fragmented over time and the reunion of people that have not seen each other in years can create its own kind of stress.

Then the funeral cortege will arrive, and as the conductor approaches the chapel, the shocking realisation that a loved one has gone forever often hits people very hard. Everyone will be focused on the final farewell.

Eventually, when the minister or celebrant announces the location of the wake during his closing remarks, there will be a sense of relief and anticipation among the mourners.

People have given up their time, gone out of their way and experienced their own personal degree of stress. Organising a wake is a lovely gesture for those that have given their support at a sad time.

The Venue

Choosing an appropriate venue will naturally depend on your budget and how much is left over in the kitty after the funeral bill. Below are some options:

- Option 1: Home. Offer some refreshments at home, particularly if there is only a small group. A neatly laid-out buffet with teas, coffees, a variety of soft drinks or alcohol should cater for everyone's needs. A stiff drink usually does the trick for numbing the nerves. If the idea of organising the catering for a home wake is too complicated with all the other arrangements under way, commission an outdoor catering company to do it for you.
- Option 2: A pub or local venue. When you have estimated how many people are likely to attend the wake, you will be able to tell whether you need to hire a function room, or whether booking an area of a pub or restaurant would suffice. A party of 20 or less, for example, will fit comfortably into an average-sized pub, and there will be no necessity to hire a function room. With larger parties it becomes more necessary to have an area set aside for a buffet.

Some of your guests may be unfamiliar with the area and will be extremely disappointed if they are unable to locate the venue of the wake. A map with straightforward directions could be handed out to your guests or illustrated on the order of service sheets.

The quality of each venue and their prices will vary greatly around the country and it is definitely worth checking out the venue in person before making a booking. Most reputable places have websites and invite people to write reviews. If they are busy they will need an approximate idea of how many people you are expecting to attend and might require a deposit to secure your booking.

Alternatively, encourage people to choose a meal from the menu and suggest that everyone goes Dutch.

Chapter 16

Religious Beliefs and Funeral Styles

At last, we have arrived at possibly the biggest and most diverse subject imaginable: religious beliefs, *and* they are more diverse than you think.

Philosophers, academics, scientists and theologians have argued the existence of God for thousands of years. Such arguments are based on the disciplines of:

1. Epistemology: the study of the nature and scope of knowledge.
2. Ontology: the study of the nature of being, existence and reality.
3. Theory of value: the belief in perfection connected to the notion of God.

Philosophical discussions about the existence of God began in the West by Plato and Aristotle, who produced cosmological arguments. This gave rise to the field of theodicy to try and establish an answer about the existence of God.

Atheists maintain that arguments for the existence of God do not provide sufficient reason to believe. On the other hand, the Catholic church maintains that knowledge of the existence of God can be proven through the natural light of human reason.

Albert Einstein once said that "Buddhists are more accepting of people and their religions. If you are totally accepting of each and every religion, you must be a Buddhist."Buddhism does not concern itself with the existence of God in any way, and Einstein believed that "If there was any religion that could cope with modern scientific needs, it would be Buddhism".

Our inherent nature makes us optimistic and hopeful of maintaining, or striving to achieve a better future, and the majority of us follow a faith of some sort. Yet the pessimistic viewpoint of religion predicts that when we lose our faith, our worlds become completely pointless because we will have no afterlife. The power of religion can never be underestimated, and each one has a deep impact on our societies.

Religions are a collection of beliefs, cultural systems, and views that relate humanity to spirituality, and sometimes to moral values. Many religions follow narratives, symbols, traditions and sacred histories that try to offer the meaning of life, or explain the origin of life and the universe. Their primary aim is to establish morality, ethics, religious laws or a preferred lifestyle from their ideas about the universe and human nature.

Despite the diversities and complexities of religious beliefs, many perform the eviction of demons, or other unwanted spiritual entities, through exorcism. Exorcism is dealt with differently, depending on the religious faith of the exorcist, but the scientific view does not allow the presence of demonic possession. The scientific point of view reasons that the symptoms associated with demonic possession can be explained as forms of mental illness, such as hysteria, mania, psychosis, Tourette's syndrome, epilepsy, schizophrenia or dissociative identity disorder.

Notable exorcisms have included:

Mother Teresa allegedly underwent an exorcism under the direction of Henry D'Souza, the Archbishop of Calcutta, who noticed that she was extremely agitated in her sleep, fearing that she "might be under the attack of an evil one".

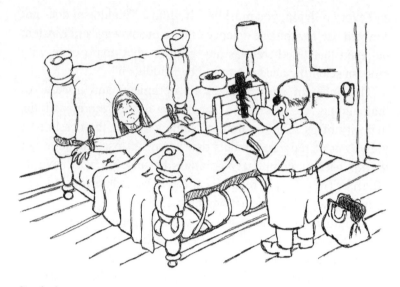

Statistics:
(According to Wikipedia)

- There are approximately 4,200 religions around the world.
- About 59% of the world's population is religious.
- About 23% of the world's population is non-religious.
- About 13% of the world's population is atheist.

(According to Pew Research Religion & Public Life Project)

The five largest groups of religion are:

Christianity	2 billion	33% of world population
Islam	1.2 billion	19.6% of world population
Hinduism	811 million	13.4% of world population
Chinese folk	385 million	6.4% of world population
Buddhism	360 million	5.9% of world population

Every new decade brings with it another new religion. For example, in 1974 Raelism was created, with the teachings that aliens created humans. It is numerically the world's largest UFO religion.

A chart that illustrates at a glance the main differences and similarities of religious beliefs is available at: www.religionfacts. com/big_religion_chart.htm

Christian Funerals

A Christian funeral marks the end of someone's life on earth. A funeral service in a parish church or crematorium chapel takes, on average, 25 minutes. During this period a mixture of blessings, psalms, hymns and prayers may be added to a eulogy, reflecting the deceased's personality with details of their journey through life.

Jewish Funerals

Jewish funerals are simple and respectful. They take place at a synagogue or at a graveside. Psalms are chanted before the eulogy is given, celebrating and honouring the deceased's life. Jewish people are buried in Jewish cemeteries and the casket is carried to the graveside by pallbearers who stop seven times whilst mourners follow. As the burial takes place, the Kaddish is recited.

Hindi Funerals

Hindus consider a funeral as the final ritual of life (samskar). Cremation of the body is almost always compulsory because it is their belief that all five elements (earth, water, fire, air and space) are returned to the earth when cremated remains are poured into the river Ganges, or into the sea. Ideally, the body should be cremated within 24 hours of death to prevent hindering the deceased's passage to the afterlife. However, in Britain, Hindi families are subject to the same statutory cremation papers that require two independent doctor's medical examinations. The body is decorated with garlands and sandalwood.

A Hindu priest conducts all of the funeral rites and, traditionally, mourning of the deceased lasts for 12 days. Hindu families may choose to witness the start of the cremation process.

Sikh Funerals

Sikhs view death as the separation of the soul from the body. From there, the soul moves on to meet the ultimate soul - God.

Cremation funerals are the accepted way for the disposal of a deceased person. The body is bathed and dressed in fresh clothes and at the crematorium a prayer known as the Kirtan Sohila is chanted and male mourners are required to wear black headscarves, whilst women wear white headscarves. Immediate family members escort the deceased to the crematorium because they will later witness the committal of the coffin into the cremator afterwards.

Mourning can take up to five weeks.

Muslim Funerals

Muslim funerals are always burials. Only men are permitted to attend a Muslim burial and only men can place a body into the grave. Although the location of a grave is allowed, the construction of a monument on top of the grave is not.

Buddhist Funerals

The death of a Buddhist marks the transition to a mode of existence within the round of rebirths. Many Buddhists believe that cremation sets the deceased's soul free, enabling it to be reborn. Mourning takes up to 100 days.

New Orleans Jazz Funerals

A typical jazz funeral begins with the family and friends of the deceased leaving a house, a funeral home or church and following a jazz band to a cemetery. As the procession advances, the band plays sombre dirges. When the ceremony has been completed, mourners proceed to a gathering place where the solemn music is replaced by some loud, raucous music and dancing. Onlookers are allowed to join in to celebrate the life of the deceased.

Green Funerals

The deceased at a green burial may be buried in an all-natural bio-degradable burial shroud, or a simple coffin constructed of cardboard, bamboo or other bio-degradable material. Their final resting place may be at a woodland burial ground or an eco-cemetery.

Top tip: Hug a tree for free, or become a Buddhist.

PART 3

LOGISTICS & LEGALITIES

Chapter 17

The Removal and Transportation of a Body

Before the Body Can Be Moved

The removal of a deceased person is a very straightforward procedure, providing there is no necessity for a coroner to become involved. When somebody passes away, the death must be confirmed as quickly as possible, regardless of whether the funeral is to be a cremation or burial, by a medical practitioner (or locum, if the death has occurred out of hours).

A Certificate of Death can be issued, along with a document granting authority to remove a deceased person, as long as the medical practitioner is satisfied that the deceased had died from natural causes, and that the death did not occur:

1. Suddenly
2. Suspiciously
3. As a result of suicide

At this point, anyone (a funeral director, next of kin of friend/ family member) can legally remove a deceased person, whether from a care home, a hospital, a bedroom or any other location, to the chosen place of rest.

Rigor mortis does not usually occur within the first 12 hours. The body must be kept in a cool and well-ventilated room to reduce the potential release of pathogens until arrangements have been made to either refrigerate or embalm the body.

The GP

Once the body has been removed, arrangements will need to be made for the deceased's usual GP to examine the body if there is to be a cremation (in the case of a burial, no doctors' certificates are required). Doctors are used to visiting funeral homes for the purpose of:

1. Making a thorough examination of the deceased
2. Completing cremation papers (part 4-5)
3. Collecting their fees (refer to Chapter 19: Doctor's Fees)

If the deceased is more than a couple of miles away from the medical practitioner's surgery, they will ask why it is so far away and why you have not contacted a local practitioner. Although any family representative or funeral home can contact the doctor's surgery, it is a legal requirement to obtain doctors' signatures for the completion of cremation papers. These days it is hard enough to persuade a doctor to make a home visit and see a patient when they are living. To avoid putting a doctor out, simply offer to take the deceased along to their practice. Suddenly, they will become much more obliging.

Contrary to belief, you will not be charged for any 'inter-county' fees whilst transporting a deceased person. However, toll charges still apply in the normal way if you are using, for example, the Severn Bridge.

DIY Transportation

There is nothing illegal about transporting a deceased person whom you are planning to cremate or bury, so long as you have:

1. A certificate of death that that has been signed by a GP
2. A removal certificate from a hospital (if applicable)
3. A transporting shell, or any item that will discreetly obscure the deceased from view
4. An estate car or van

Discretion and dignity are integral factors for the removal and transportation of any deceased person.

Chapter 18
Doctor's Fees (Ash Cash)

"Doctor! Did you even notice the dagger between Mr Norman's shoulder blades?"

These days families prefer to cremate their loved one's rather than bury them, according to the Cremation Society of Great Britain's statistics .There are several reasons for this such as cost, the perception of it being more efficient and cleaner, and the fact that they are far less bother than tending a grave on a renewable lease.

The previous chapter explained the Certificate of Death. After this has been issued and the deceased transported to the chosen place of rest, then the cremation papers must be completed.

Cremation Applications

Applications for cremation are mandatory, regardless as to whether they are represented by a funeral director, or by a personal application, and their charges are unavoidable. Application forms are available from all crematoriums and the following tips are important to note:

1. Always use a black ballpoint pen.
2. Only return the original documents. Photocopies, emails and faxes will not be accepted.
3. Signed cremation documents must be sent to the crematorium at least three days before the date of the funeral for examination. Otherwise the cremation will not be allowed to go ahead.

The world is full of red tape and at times the funeral industry is no exception. For application form examples, please refer to Chapter 7: Choosing a Crematorium.

The Doctor and His Fee

This is affectionately known in the trade as 'ash cash', although judging by the speed that most doctors conduct their 'examinations' it might as well be re-named: 'dash cash'.

But despite doctors' fees being passed on to the family as a 'third party cost', cremations remain a cheaper arrangement option than earth burials.

Firstly, the GP whom your loved one was registered with prior to death must fill in part 1.

Secondly, the cremation documentation requires a second medical practitioner to complete: Medical Certificate part 4 and 5, and also to check that part 1 of the documentation is correct.

On 31st January 2000, Dr Harold Frederick Shipman made history when he was convicted of at least 250 murders that were positively ascribed to him. After his life sentence, an enquiry was launched and much of Britain's legal structure concerning healthcare and medicine were reviewed and modified, as a result of his crimes. This exposed the obvious downfall of having just one doctor sign a certificate where a body, possibly full of incriminating DNA, is cremated.

This is necessary because a body cannot be examined after a cremation has taken place. All DNA evidence is totally destroyed, unlike a burial where the body can be exhumed at a later date for examination, should foul play be suspected.

Most doctors conduct their examinations during NHS time and are required to fill in the cremation papers, parts 4 and 5, by invitation to a funeral home mortuary. Although a thorough examination is a legal requirement to establish the exact cause of death, it is usually conducted by nothing more than a casual glance at the deceased's ID tag. This will remain attached to the wrist or ankle at all times and states the deceased's name; a date and time of death; and hospital details where applicable.

In cases where a doctor feels unsure that the particulars entered in part 1 of the cremation papers are incorrect, or notices something untoward, the coroner must be informed by law (refer to Chapter 20: The Coroner).

Mortuary assistants and embalmers can only proceed with an embalming operation when parts 4 and 5 of the cremation papers have been fully completed (refer to Chapter 14: Embalming – is it really necessary?).

The new legislation was designed to bring confidence back to the cremation system and families are now allowed to inspect their loved one's cremation papers, if they so wish.

Top tip: In the case of a cremation funeral, if your loved one has been referred to a coroner for a post mortem examination, you will not be charged any doctors' fees. A coroner's certificate of examination overrides a medical examination by a GP.

The bereavement office, located in most hospital, will prepare all the cremation documentation along with the doctors' signatures for you

Chapter 19

The Coroner

According to the coroners' average statistics, 46 % of all deaths in the UK are referred to the coroner's office. A coroner is a government official who investigates and determines a cause of death. They are authorised to issue death certificates, maintain death records, respond to deaths in mass disasters and identify unknown dead bodies.

In most cases, the coroner determines the cause of death personally, otherwise junior assistants investigate cases whilst the coroner presides at a special court.

The History of The Coroner & The Law

It is in the interest of a community that sudden, unnatural or unexplained deaths are investigated. The role of the coroner was first established in 1194 as an independent judicial officer charged with investigating sudden, violent or unnatural deaths. Early coroners investigated anything that was potentially beneficial for collecting revenue for the Crown. Suicides were classified as 'self-murder', therefore the goods and chattels of a suicide victim would fall forfeit to the Crown. Similarly with victims of disasters at sea, any buried treasure became 'treasure trove'. Over eight centuries later, this is still one of the coroner's duties.

'Treasure trove' is defined as any object, or group of objects, that are discovered and identified as being over 300 years old and contain 10% or more of gold, or silver.

After the Norman Conquest, local communities were deterred from killing Normans with a heavy fine levied on an entire village where a dead body was discovered, as it was assumed that any dead body was Norman unless it could be proved that the body was English. The fine was known as the *Murdrem*, derived from the word 'murder'. Early coroner's inquests dealt with the "Presumption of Normandy", which could only be disputed by the local community to avoid a fine, by the "Presentment of Englishry".

The coroner system adapted over the centuries, but it was not until the 19th century that major changes occurred relating to the investigation of deaths in the community. The first Births and Deaths Registration Act was introduced in 1836, prompted by public concern and panic caused by inaccurate records of the actual numbers of deaths caused from epidemics, such as cholera.

The Coroners Society of England and Wales was formed in 1846 and Sergeant William Payne became HM Coroner for Southwark and the City of London.

The Coroners Act of 1887 made significant changes to the way murder cases were investigated. Coroners were concerned with determining the circumstances and the actual medical causes of sudden, violent and unnatural deaths for the benefit of the community, whereas they had previously remained unchallenged.

These days, the coroner responds to and investigates deaths that have been referred for a wide variety of reasons. Over one third of all deaths in England and Wales are currently referred to the coroner. The law does not allow the screening of all deaths that occur in the community, or in a hospital, and it is for the coroner to decide which deaths should be investigated. However, in light of the Harold Shipman enquiry, the law might change.

On 22nd May 2012, the first Chief Coroner of England and Wales announced that he had overseen the implementation of The Coroner and Justice Act 2009, which was implemented in July 2013. The Act provides a number of structural changes to the coroner's system, including the introduction of a new concept of investigations into deaths, removing existing barriers, creating new titles for coroners, and providing for a new system of death certification (by medical examiners).

The Office of Coroner has survived for over 800 years and is likely to continue evolving to meet the changing needs of society.

If your loved one has been referred to the coroner's office and you have booked a cremation funeral through a funeral director, you will not be charged any doctors' fees (refer to Chapter 19: Doctor's Fees) because the coroner's certificate overrides the decision of any medical practitioner.

Top tip: Inspect the cremation papers, sections 4 and 5, and disagree with your findings? The case will automatically be referred to the coroner, negating the doctors' fees.

The coroner's '14 day rule' states that: when someone has passed away and had not been seen by their usual medical practitioner within a 14 day period prior to death, that the coroner must automatically be called, and to establish whether or not to proceed with a post mortem examination. This procedure could even happen in cases where the death was expected. During end of life stages, district nurses may decide to call out the patient's doctor, even in cases where there is nothing more that the doctor could possibly do to prevent the death from occurring. The logic of having a doctor in attendance

towards the end should technically prevent any involvement from the coroner. Unfortunately not all doctors oblige to attend.

Chapter 20

The State Funeral (Pauper's Funeral) & Bereavement Payments

In England, a pauper's funeral refers to a funeral for a homeless person, or for someone without an available next of kin to fund their funeral, or someone whose family cannot afford it. Over time, families have become more scattered than ever before and consequently lose touch with their relatives. There are many cases where the state is left to pay for a basic funeral.

Local authorities are duty-bound under section 46 of the Public Health (Control of Diseases) Act 1984 to fund the funeral costs where family members cannot be traced. Public money is used to perform the most simplistic funerals. They are always arranged as cremations because the cost is less than a burial.

This type of funeral is put out to tender by the councils to their local funeral directors to reduce costs further. Although family and friends are allowed to attend the funeral, nobody has any say in its timing, or any other aspect of the arrangement.

The coffin is delivered to the crematorium by van, usually before 9.30a.m., and before the start of any listed and planned services. It will have been placed on the catafalque regardless of anyone turning up, and the attending minister will perform a brief blessing without music. The entire service could be over within a few minutes if there are no mourners present.

Statistically, more men are likely to be provided with a state funeral than women.

Bereavement Payments

If your spouse or civil partner has died, you may be eligible for a bereavement payment. This is a one-off, tax-free, lump sum payment of £2,000.

To be eligible for payment your spouse or civil partner must have:

1. Paid National Insurance contributions. However, if your spouse's death had been caused by their job it does not matter whether they paid National Insurance contributions or not.
2. Not been entitled to Category A State Retirement Pension when they died.
3. Below state pension age when they died.

You will not receive a bereavement payment if:

1. You were divorced, or had dissolved your civil partnership when your spouse died.
2. You are living with another person as husband, wife, or civil partner.
3. You are in prison.

If you believe you are eligible but had already emigrated when the death occurred, you must contact the International Pension Centre to find out if you can claim after you have moved abroad.

Contact details:

The Bereavement Service contact details are:

Telephone: 0845 606 0265 Monday to Friday 8.00a.m. – 6.00p.m.

The Department for Work & Pensions

Bereavement and widow's benefits

International Pension Centre

Tyneview Park

Newcastle Upon Tyne

NE98 1BA

Telephone: + 44 (0)191 21 87608

NB: Remember to have your National Insurance number ready when you call.

Form BB1 (Bereavement Benefit pack) is available from all local Jobcentre Plus offices. When you have completed Form BB1 you must return it to Jobcentre Plus as soon as possible for processing.

Chapter 21

The Importance of
Making a Will

Anyone can make a will, regardless of their circumstances. People who make a will do so for peace of mind when the inevitable happens. A will is written to determine the distribution of a person's assets. The owner of the will, who states their wishes for asset distribution after death may be married, divorced, single, separated or living with a partner.

Contesting a Will

After death, the will content may be called into question if one or more family members thinks that the assets were unfairly divided, or if there are grounds to claim it invalid. A will contest, in the law of property, is a formal rejection raised against the validity of a will, based on the contention that the will does not reflect the intent of the testator (the person who actually made the will). Will contests are generally based on the assertion that the testator lacked testamentary capacity, was deluded, or subject to fraud. In any of these circumstances a will may be contested.

There are two categories of people who can legally contest a will.

1. The beneficiaries (the person or people named in the will)
2. Anyone who would inherit from the testator if the will was invalid

Common Grounds and Reasons for Contesting a Will

Claims against the testator's lack of mental capacity (state of mind and memory loss) are the most common testamentary challenges. For a will to be valid, a testator must have sufficient mental ability to comprehend: the amount and nature of his/her property, the family members and loved ones who would ordinarily receive such property by Last Will and Testament, and how his/her Last Will and Testament disposes of such property.

Just because a testator may have been suffering from a form of mental illness or disease does not mean that he/she did not have the requisite mental capacity to prepare a Last Will and Testament. Competency to execute a Last Will and Testament generally means that the testator understood the nature and extent of his/her assets and knew who the benefactors are.

In cases where a testator appeared to have lacked mental capacity when executing a Last Will and Testament, proof must be provided via medical records (e.g. proving insane delusions), and reports of behaviour from those close to the deceased.

If it is suspected that the will was made under duress, e.g. some threat of physical harm or coercion caused the execution of the will, then the will can be contested.

Fraud has four general categories:

1. False representations of material facts to the testator
2. Knowledge by the perpetrator that the representations are false
3. Intent that the representations be acted upon
4. Resulting injury

The two primary types of fraud are:

1. Fraud in the execution
2. Fraud in the inducement

Top tip: Although anyone can make a legally-binding will, it is advisable to have one drawn up by a solicitor and kept in their safe hands.

Chapter 22

Probate

The term 'probate' refers to a legal documentation and is the first stage in the legal process of administering the estate of a deceased person. Its purpose is to distribute the deceased's property, written under a will (refer to Chapter 22: The Importance of Making a Will).

Probate may be officially appointed to: a family solicitor, a member of the family or even a family friend. The named executor will be written into the will, which also becomes a legal document and may have to be enforced through a court in the case of any disputes. The person named as executor in the will also has legal power to dispose of the testator's assets, as stated within the will.

If there is no will, the process is much more complicated and an *Application for a Grant of Administration* document must be obtained from a court. This allows administrators to proceed with administrating probate.

Key Points

PR (Personal Representative): Any executor or administrator.

Grants of Representation: Some banks and other financial organisations require a grant of representation before allowing access to any money. A grant of representation is not required for estates left by the deceased under £5,000, or when everything was owned jointly with someone else.

It is required for: sums in excess of £5,000; cases involving stocks and shares; property or land; and for insurance policies.

A grant can be obtained by a solicitor, or in person at:

The Principal Registry (Family Division) of the London Probate Registry

Telephone: 0845 302 0900

Applying in person requires an interview at the registry. They will supply you with an application form and a tax form. Registry staff will assist with the forms (fees apply).

The rules of intestacy are set out in the *Administration of Estates Act 1925*.

Inheritance Tax: Any personal representatives have to find out if any inheritance tax is due when someone has died, and if any monies owed must be paid.

Liability for inheritance tax depends on:

- The value of the property and personal belongings at the time of death.
- The value of any gifts given prior to death and whom they were given to.
- The value of any trusts that the deceased had benefited from, or the people likely to benefit under the will, or under the rules of intestacy.

For up to date information on how inheritance tax could affect you visit: www.hmrc.gov.uk

Timescales

Sorting out the estate of a deceased person can take up to a year, perhaps longer when there are complications. Many organisations may be involved with the process, such as banks, building societies, insurance companies and HM Customs & Revenue.

Where the deceased had debts, any individual seeking a claim on the estate has up to six months to make a claim after probate has been granted.

Other factors affecting timeframes include: whether or not the deceased's financial affairs were in order; what the deceased owned and where; whether the deceased had an interest in a business or a farm; the details written in the will; whether there are any legal disputes; any due inheritance tax; ensuring that HM Revenue & Customs files have been closed; as well as sorting out any pensions and benefit agency issues.

Costs

Solicitor's fees vary from company to company and are dependent on the complexities of the estate.

Top tip: Make sure you receive a written quote from your chosen solicitor before instructing them to administer your affairs, and obtain several comparative quotes before proceeding.

Chapter 23

Pre-paid Funeral Planning

An Introduction to Pre-paid Funeral Planning

The old truism *"Life's too short"* is perhaps a bit old hat when the reality for the majority of people these days is "that life really does drag" (and most of us sincerely hope that it does). We are forever striving to live longer and healthier lives. But as we do, funeral costs keep on escalating every year at an astonishing rate.

The concept of pre-paid funeral planning is a 'win-win' situation for everyone. A funeral plan, which has been accredited to a funeral director, guarantees future work for them when the plan holder eventually passes away. The individuals that are left behind are saved the worry of funeral debt, as well as any funeral director's inflationary costs. The difference between funeral plans is not always apparent to anyone that has not analysed them in detail. In simple terms, a funeral plan is a way of paying for a future funeral today.

What a Funeral Plan Covers

Itemised within each funeral plan are the type of vehicles, including how many are required; the type of coffin including specific designs; the name of the crematorium or cemetery. Special instructions may be written into the plan to include music choices; floral arrangements; preferred minister or celebrant; dove or balloon release; venue for refreshments.

Funeral Plan Operators

There are several plan operators that different funeral directors' groups link themselves to:

1. Dignity Pre Arrangement Ltd, a subsidiary of Dignity plc. The Age UK Guaranteed Funeral Plan is offered by Advanced Planning Ltd, which is also owned by Dignity plc.

2. Co-operative Funeralcare link their pre-paid funeral plans to Sun Life Funeral Plans and Sun Life Direct.

3. NFFD offer consumer funeral plans through SafeHands. SafeHands funeral plans claim to be the most affordable funeral plan provider, which means the consumer pays less. The administration charge is only 1% to funeral directors selling the plans, which are thought to be significantly cheaper than any of their competitors. They do not have an 'in-house' salesforce to promote themselves and are therefore promoted more softly through national will writers, IFAs, solicitors and sales firms. A key difference with a SafeHands funeral plan is that people can buy a funeral plan cheaply without allocating the funds to a specific funeral director until the time of death, rather than when it was first written in advance of the client's death. SafeHands are self-regulated and do not have to be endorsed by any governing body. By remaining independent, SafeHands are able to pass on their savings to their customers.

Types of Pre-Paid Funeral Plans:

1. Insurance linked funeral plans: Life insurance policies (also known as 'over-50's' plans) pay out a lump sum on the death of the policy holder. The cost can be spread over a long period of time, but you may end up paying more in premiums than the value of the policy at the time of your death, depending on when you die. For example, a 60 year old man that pays £15 per month into an insurance plan provider may receive the full policy value of £2,879 after two years. After his 76th birthday he would have paid out more than the policy covers and would have to continue his payments until he is 90, and beyond. His premiums may even increase with age and will, in most cases, continue until he dies.

2. Trust-funded funeral plans: A trust-funded funeral plan puts money aside allocated for the sole purpose of paying for a future funeral. The money usually remains untouched up until the time of need.

If you have selected a suitable independent funeral director for your pre-paid funeral package, your plan will cover professional services at the time of need. There will also be an administration charge added to the bottom of the bill that will be charged when the plan is first taken out. Funeral directors have no influence over any potential future inflation of the third party costs. Therefore, even though you might have paid for third party costs upfront, there will inevitably be a shortfall of funds that your family will be asked to pay for after the funeral.

Pre-Paid Funeral Plan Breakdown

Typically, a pre-paid funeral plan is broken down as follows, with each item having a maximum cost that it is covered up until:

Funeral director costs:

1. **The supply of all necessary staff and professional arrangements**
2. **Supply of a hearse and a limousine**
3. **Additional limousines**
4. **Coffin type**
5. **Ashes casket**
6. **Extras**

Third party costs:

1. **Crematorium/burial fees**
2. **Doctors' fees**
3. **Minister's fee**

Administration fee:

Total to pay:

Most funeral plan providers are governed by strict rules and abide by rigid codes of conduct. Funeral plan companies associated with the NAFD set up the National Association of Pre-Paid Funeral Planning NAPFP in 1993. The association claims to represent the majority of all plan holders. The NAPFP were instrumental in setting up the FPA, the Funeral Planning Authority, and since 2002 all members of the association are required to register with the Funeral Planning Authority.

Most funeral plan providers are likely to bombard you with persuasive slogans such as, "peace of mind", and "the most thoughtful thing you could ever do for your family". In terms of easing the financial burden for your loved ones when you're gone, they are absolutely right.

Top tip: The funeral director's costs and fees vary from company to company. Compare quotes from two or three funeral homes before committing yourself.

Pre-paid funeral planning could potentially save your family thousands of pounds, but you must consider the potential third party shortfalls at the time of need, whether they are trust-funded or insurance-linked.

Top tips:

- *Look out for funeral directors that are NFFD registered*
- *Check the NFFD funeral director register: www. funeralregister.com*
- *Compare funeral director pre-paid funeral plan quotations with SafeHands*

Chapter 24

Repatriation

Repatriation is the process of returning a deceased person to their country of origin, or current citizenship. Death can occur at any time whilst abroad. Most funeral directors offer a service that either receives, or sends out (import or export) a person that has passed away during a visit to another country. There are also a number of specialist repatriation companies that can assist with all the rules surrounding repatriation.

Their job is to liaise with the relevant embassy of the country concerned, and to sort out all of the associated red tape.

The majority of the documentation required is listed as follows:

1. An export licence is not required to repatriate a body out of the UK, although a customs entry form is required for a body to come into the country.
2. The death certificate.
3. A certificate stating that the deceased is free from infection or an embalming certificate combined with the funeral director's declaration required when a body is leaving the UK. There are some countries that require additional documentation, including the deceased's passport.
4. Customs clearance is required for any human remains entering from outside the EC.
5. Customs clearance charges sometimes apply.
6. Coffins must be zinc-lined.

7. The coffin may be required by the airline to be wrapped in hessian, protective bubble wrap, or a flight tray.

Some repatriation cases can be extremely complex. It is the one scenario where embalming a body becomes a legal requirement.

When widow Gitta Jarant and stepdaughter, Anke Anusic, checked into John Lennon airport, with the body of Curt Will Jarant on a flight bound for Berlin (6th April 2010), they insisted that the wheelchair-bound 91 year old, who was wearing sunglasses at the time, was asleep. On closer inspection, officials discovered the gentleman to be dead, and both women were arrested on suspicion of failing to give notification of death. Whenever a death occurs, the correct procedure is to obtain a certificate of death from a doctor. This is a legal requirement.

According to the women's version of events, the situation had become a sudden death" scenario because they did not know he was dead. The women would have needed to inform the police when his death became obvious and then contact the coroner's office automatically. This would have been the only way to establish an exact cause of death, record an accurate time of death, and exonerate the women from any possible wrongdoing.

"Are you OK Sir?"

Chapter 25

Exhumation

Most grave exhumations occur after suspicious circumstances have come to light following the death and subsequent burial of a person. Exhumations are extremely distressing for everyone involved, including the cemetery staff. When it becomes a matter for the police and Home Office pathologists to prove or disprove foul play, the circumstances of exhumation are beyond the family's control.

However, some exhumations occur when cemetery officials have made a burial planning mistake. An example of this is when a family has purchased a new grave in a cemetery for a two-person occupancy and the grave is not dug deep enough. The burial of the first occupant may have consisted of the internment of a cremated remains casket after a cremation rather than a coffin. The grave may only have been dug shallow enough (a couple of feet), and wide enough to take a small casket.

Years later, the family may opt to use the purchased grave as a full burial interment if a loved one had stated verbally, or had written in their will that they preferred to be buried. A special licence will be required before the burial is allowed to go ahead, for the original cremated remains casket to be legally exhumed. Then the grave will have to be re-dug deep enough, and wide enough, for the burial of a coffin and the re-burial of the cremated remains casket.

When the most elementary of mistakes occur during a burial, the consequences are extremely costly and the height of embarrassment for those concerned.

Another example includes a coffin being interred round the wrong way. Christian faith cemeteries require the head end of the coffin to enter a grave towards the headstone.

Sometimes an oversight occurs when a funeral director instructs the bearers to lower the coffin without realising that it is entering the grave back to front. The mistake may not be noticed until the gravediggers arrive to fill in, usually after the family has dispersed from the cemetery. By then it is too late to rectify the matter, and an exhumation licence is required from the Home Office before the coffin can be legally extracted and re-interned (refer to Chapter 30: Factual Anecdotes and Monumental Cock-Ups).

Another typical example of an embarrassing cemetery blunder is when a coffin begins its decent into the grave. If it becomes stuck whilst entering the grave and does not reach the bottom, the incident technically becomes a matter for the Home Office. They must authorise an exhumation and reburial. Gravediggers have to be certain that a coffin can pass to the required depth to avoid any major enquiry.

When cemeteries reach full capacity, older plots may be marked for renovation where there is no traceable contact for a family to renew their grave lease, which usually runs between 75 and 100 years. The remains will then be exhumed and moved to an ossuary to accommodate new burials, in accordance with burial contracts, religious and local authority burial laws.

Construction companies occasionally discover the location of an ancient burial site during excavations whilst digging the foundations for new buildings. These are often mass graves. In this case, the cemetery will need to be relocated. Each body will need to be exhumed and transported to the new site. Specialist exhumation companies will liaise with archaeologists enabling them to gain a better understanding of how those people had once lived and died. Sometimes their skeletal remains are found piled together, making it impossible for any formal identification.

Specialist exhumation companies are expensive to commission, but their work needs to be extremely detailed from the outset as they make a thorough site survey. Then, before any work commences, they are required to liaise with the media, members of the clergy, as well as any legal representatives. Site screens are erected around the perimeter and the documentation of the site will begin. On-site security may be round the clock whilst trees are felled and memorial headstones are removed. Any private exhumations are undertaken as quickly as possible.

When the entire site is cleared, the ground has to be levelled and compacted before an exhumation company is able to issue a Cherished Land Certificate of Completion.

Forms

Exhumation forms can be obtained from The Ministry of Justice. You will need to request an application for a licence for the removal of buried human remains (including cremated remains) in England and Wales.

PART 4

THE FINAL
FAREWELL

Chapter 26

The Service, or 'Final Event' of a Loved One's Life

Photo courtesy of: Irvin Amusements Ltd

The funeral service is often regarded as the most nerve-racking element of the entire undertaking process. The lead up to the funeral may see the funeral director and the staff achieve many great things for you whilst your loved one reposes in their care. You may even have developed some admiration for your chosen undertaker, perhaps sharing some personal memories together with a few cups of coffee.

But now everything hinges on the minister or celebrant arriving at the chosen venue.

Anecdote No.1

A minister arrives at Reading Crematorium with just seconds to spare before the beginning of the service. The funeral director gives him a puzzled look, to which the minister says, "How long do you think it takes to get from Basingstoke to Reading?" The funeral director shrugs his shoulders, and reckons it takes a good 45 minutes.

"I managed it in exactly 21 minutes," replied the minister, still pumping with adrenalin. "I only went to the wrong bloody crematorium, didn't I?!"

Anecdote No.2

One day, a minister was booked to take a funeral at a crematorium that he had never travelled to before. A worrying amount of rain came down that morning and the traffic was inevitably atrocious. So, to be on the safe side, he put the address of where he was going to into his satnav and went on his way.

The traffic was much worse than he had anticipated. When he eventually arrived and parked up in the crematorium car park he only had five minutes to spare. But at least he was there and would be able to conduct the service without the embarrassment of being late. Placing everything that was of value into his briefcase, he walked briskly across the carpark to the attendant's office where he was able to compose himself, switch off his mobile phone and check that everything was ready. He then walked over to the lectern, placed his briefcase on the floor and retrieved his notes to deliver his service.

Soon the chapel was packed with mourners, the coffin was placed onto the catafalque, and after the entry music had faded out he was ready to begin.

At that moment a voice coming from the briefcase next to his feet said, "You have now reached your final destination." In his haste he had forgotten to switch off his trusty satnav.

We are all human and everyone makes mistakes. The obvious questions that will be running through an undertaker's mind on arrival include:

- Will the Minister turn up on time?
- Will he/she overrun with the allotted service time? (25 minutes on average)
- Has he/she met with the family?
- Has he/she done their homework?

Last Minute Preparations

A funeral director will have made any last minute preparations over the course of the previous evening.

He would probably have anticipated the mood and general attitude of the family with a courteous "Are we all set for tomorrow?" chat over the phone, or the family may even have received a personal knock at the door. He will also endeavour to pre-empt anything that is likely to impede the funeral or cause delay, such as the curse of road works en-route to the venue. Whatever physical or psychological obstacles may have sprung up overnight, the funeral director must remain cool, calm and collected, just as he had been during the first point of contact with the family. Anything less would be paramount to failure.

A funeral director knows all too well the importance of arriving on time and how discourteous arriving late would be, even by a couple of minutes. Families always feel considerable pressure just before a funeral and will not accept slack punctuality for any reason.

Limousines will pick up the close family members as arranged, and when the family is comfortably inside, the journey will commence...

The Service Itself

These days anything within reason is acceptable during a funeral service and it is up to the family what type of content they would like added.

A more traditional service requires a minister for all aspects of religion. However, when it comes to the eulogy, a lot of ministers barely make much reference to the deceased. Instead they prefer to wrap the entire funeral ceremony around a basic religious format: opening prayer; hymn; another prayer; another hymn; the committal and The Lord's Prayer followed by a blessing.

A celebrant would not begin until the entry music has completely faded. Then, after a brief welcome and introduction, a detailed resume and the celebration of life begins. This includes when and where a deceased was born; childhood scenarios and historical timelines; their adolescence and first jobs, including any hobbies and interests; as well as their unique personality traits. Anecdotal detail invariably covers when they dated their marital partner (if applicable), leading to the introduction of a sentimental piece of music chosen by the family. This allows mourners to reflect on the deceased's life halfway through the service. The chronological timeline continues during the second half of the service where children and additional family members are also included within the eulogy script; family holidays and memorable occasions are discussed; family members can be invited to offer their own personal tributes if they wish, or to read a poem of their choice . The essence of the deceased's character can be highlighted whilst finalising the service and before the exit music is introduced. Many other elements can be added by prior arrangement with the family, such as the inclusion of any prayers; donations to a charity; an invitation to join the family for refreshments (or wake).

Top tips:

- *Organise your own eulogy, using your own choice of music, poems, and personal tributes – without the expense of booking a minister or celebrant.*
- *If you are booking a celebrant or a Humanist, make sure that you get a quote first. Some will charge extortionate fees.*

Chapter 27

Ways to Enhance a Funeral Service

info@celebrantsociety.org.uk

This company would appear extremely flexible for life celebrations http://www.celebrantsociety.org.uk/

Below are some of the nicest touches that can be included at funerals:

1: Photograph

It is always a nice idea to have a framed photograph (no smaller than A5 for visibility) of your loved one on display, either on the coffin or nearby. A DVD playing a montage of photographs throughout the decades of life is a gentle way of helping people reflect on someone's life during the service.

2: Written Messages

A blank coffin (without handles) containing your loved one, resting on a pair of trestles at the front of the chapel for easy access, provides a blank canvass for some uplifting interaction with your mourners. Why not bring a bag of indelible markers along with you to hand out when your own personal tribute has finished?

Gently bring the service to an end by saying:

"I would like to thank you all for your support and for joining us here for today's ceremony, and by paying your respects to: 'deceased's name'."

Everyone will appreciate the invitation and opportunity to stand with you by the coffin. Allowing mourners to scribble their own personalised messages of love over a section of the coffin can be extremely uplifting, and memorable.

You could also add:

"... and your written messages of love will go with 'deceased's name', as we say our final farewells before leaving."

3: Personal Artwork or Music

If your loved one had been an accomplished artist or musician, display an example of their work, or any personal items, for everyone to see. It will reflect a splash of their personality and will remain as a vivid reminder for everyone.

4: Roses

Take a bunch of roses with you so that immediate family members can walk up and place them on the coffin during the service, or whilst some music is playing. Make sure that all the thorns have been removed from each rose stems before the funeral.

5: Closing of Curtains

The closing of curtains has been a traditional way to end a cremation service and the procedure is still preferred by ministers. Unfortunately, many people say they are unhappy to see them close because it is too final. It becomes the most loathed part of the service because of the barrier that it creates between the family and their loved one. People's perceptions of what happens to the coffin once the curtains have closed varies considerably. There is no overall right or wrong option as some people find having the curtains closed offers them a form of comfort.

Regardless of the style of service that you choose, religious or otherwise, ask your minister to leave the curtains open throughout the ceremony if it is your preference. The decision is yours to make and not the minister's. If you tell your funeral arranger what you have decided before the funeral, they will ensure your wishes are respected; although some ministers may take a lot of convincing.

6: Personal Readings

Ask the celebrant or minister to welcome and introduce the service and allow your family members to recall their own personal anecdotes, tributes and special readings. In a similar way, the celebrant or minister could simply conclude with a brief characterisation, a prayer, announcement of the venue for refreshments, and to then announce the exit music. The celebrant or minister can work with you as your master of ceremonies and take a more 'back seat' role if the family want to be more involved.

7: Brandy

When the exit music is playing, advise your conductor if you prefer to remain inside the chapel until the very end of your chosen piece of music. Then, produce a heart-warming bottle of brandy (or any other favourite choice), and invite everyone to enjoy a shot as your final 'fond farewell' gesture to a loved one.

8: Record it

Arrange to have an audio recording of the service as your own keepsake, or to enable you to send a copy to those unable to attend.

Similarly, a film recording of the service is a lovely way to remember someone's final event. Although filming is more technical and can be expensive, it would be advisable to obtain comparative quotes first.

Ask your celebrant or minister to supply or email you a copy of the written eulogy.

9: Donations Box

Organise a donations box. You may instruct your funeral director to place a donations box by the exit door for people to see when they are leaving. People can make a donation towards the charity of your choice if they want to.

Every charity is registered and numbered, and you can easily track how much money had been raised after a particular funeral with the charity concerned.

10: Christmas Funerals

If the funeral of a loved one falls during Christmas week, request a cheerful Christmas carol for one of your music choices.

11: Gay Funerals

Choose a fast, upbeat disco track for your exit music and wait until your celebrant or minister announces it. Then produce a bottle of pink liquid glitter, slap it on your forehead and run it through your hair to symbolise your loved one's world as a fun mark of respect. Then pass it on to the next mourner. You can then dance away as though you were at a nightclub, and whilst the glitter is being passed round, more people get up to join in with the dancing. Any tearfulness is guaranteed to subside at this point, as you transform a sombre occasion into a joyous celebration of life. Be as flamboyant as you dare. The conductor is unlikely to put a stop to you all enjoying yourselves.

After the Service

Thoughtful additions:

1. A dove release. When doves are released in the cemetery gardens, it provides a beautiful and serene way to end any funeral. White doves are symbolic of peace and love, and as they encircle the grounds before returning home, they will provide comfort to most.

2. A balloon release. This is perhaps the least expensive of all post-service events, but it is an effective way of emphasising the love that everyone felt towards someone.

3. Fireworks. Send your loved one's cremated remains into the air attached to some fireworks in the privacy of your garden, or a quiet, memorable location.

Chapter 28

Bereavement Counselling and the Truth About Tranquillizers

The death of a loved one is a sad time for anyone, regardless of how the person has died. The complexities of bereavement counselling are dependent on many factors, including the circumstances of how a loved one passed away. When someone experiences grief they experience a series of interchangeable emotions, particularly if a personal bond had been formed. It can also impact heavily on a person's physical, cognitive and behavioural dimensions.

In general terms:
'Bereavement' refers to the state of loss.
'Grief' refers to the reaction of loss.

The loss of a loved one makes people grieve beyond any other type of loss, such as losing a job or of any material possessions. Overcoming the loss of a loved one takes time, and for some, it feels like a total impossibility. Grief and how it is perceived by the griever depends on: our age; state of mind at the time of loss; the circumstances of death and whether or not it was expected; other people around us at the time and how the news has affected them; how busy we are; how rational or levelheaded our personalities are, and so on.

The Four Steps

Although the process differs for everyone, there is a general four-step model:

1. Shock and denial:

Bad news can overwhelm us and sometimes our natural instinct is not to believe what we are being told, even though, subconsciously, we know that it is true. A state of denial could last for several weeks.

2. Thoughts invaded:

The death of a loved one has such a finality that for many, the entire situation of the loss will invade our thoughts during ordinary conversations, or whilst performing everyday tasks. The invasion of thoughts can last for many months.

3. Depression:

This is the longest process because it involves accepting the reality of having lost somebody. The state of depression might include intense feelings of anger, guilt, sadness or anxiety.

4. Recovery:

The recovery period is all about picking up the pieces and feeling more enthusiastic about performing daily tasks, joining in with others socially, achieving goals, and enjoying a new sense of well-being.

This probably sounds a bit 'tick box' because the circumstances relating to the death of a loved one are so variable. The death of a child could occur during childbirth, which of course is very traumatic. However, if the death occurs when the child is slightly older, it is likely to prove incomparable to any other form of loss where the parents are concerned.

When life has become too unbearable for someone, to the point where they commit suicide, its impact will be everlasting and deeply felt by the entire family.

The loss of a partner or spouse is also extremely powerful because the person that died had become part of someone else's life to the point where they may not understand how to "go it alone". Years of doing things together and having separate duties within the home are suddenly changed forever.

To lose a brother, sister or other sibling is unique in its severity of impact, particularly for twins that have known each other since birth. The significance of losing a sibling shifts the entire hierarchy within a family unit. However, when siblings were not on good terms with each other, then feelings of guilt may be severely felt.

The loss of an elder family member is perhaps an easier situation to process because when an elderly person passes away it is usually because they had reached the end of their life, or natural causes. Although their loss is a sad one, it is also a natural occurrence and part of the process of life, and some elderly people may even welcome the concept of death if they have been suffering, or lacking in any quality of life.

Counselling

Care must be taken whenever choosing a bereavement counsellor because everyone's circumstances of grief are so unique. The counsellor should be adequately qualified with sufficient experience that relates to your situation.

Below are a few helpful starting points for finding an excellent bereavement counsellor:

Bereavement organisations include:

Bereavement Advice Centre
Tel: 0800 634 9494
www.bereavementadvice.org.uk

CRUSE Bereavement Care
126 Sheen Road
Richmond TW91UR
Tel: 020 8939 9534
email: helpline@crusebereavementcare.org.uk
www.crusebereavement.org.uk

London Bereavement Network
356 Holloway Road
London N7 6PA
Tel: 020 7700 8134
email: info@bereavement.org.uk
www.bereavement.org.uk

SANDS (Stillbirth And Neonatal Death Society)
28 Portland Place
London W1B 1LY
Tel: (Helpline) 020 7436 5881
Tel: (Admin) 020 7436 3715
www.uk-sands.org

The Samaritans
The Upper Mill
Kingston Road
Ewell

Surrey KT17 2AF
Tel: 020 8394 8300
email: admin@samaritans.org
www.samaritans.org

Age UK
Tavis House
1-6 Tavistock Square
London WC1H 9NA
Tel: 0800 169 6565
www.ageuk.org.uk

Child Bereavement Network
Clare Charity Centre
Wycombe Road
Saunderton
Buckinghamshire HP14 4HU
Tel: 01494 568900
www.childbereavement.org.uk

Survivors of Bereavement by Suicide
The Flamsteed Centre
Albert Street
Ilkeston
Derbyshire DE7 5GU
Tel: 0115 944 1117
www.uk-sobs.org.uk

Top tip: Most individuals and organisations specialising in bereavement counselling are highly professional and caring. Some charge a fee whilst others do not. Phone around first because overcoming the loss of a loved one may require numerous visits to a counsellor.

Tranquillisers

Tranquillisers have their role too. However, they are not the overall solution and can be addictive. Tranquillisers such as Valium and Ativan are designed to help people relax and take life at a slower pace. But after a while people tend to build up a tolerance (or resistance) towards them. Then higher doses will be needed more frequently to gain the same effect. The process of breaking the habit becomes extremely difficult and can trigger some major side effects. Other side effects include a vicious cycle of: short term memory loss, anxiety, drowsiness, tremors, vomiting, panic attacks, epileptic fits, and depression. If mixed with alcohol, tranquillisers form a lethal cocktail that can kill.

PART 5

FUNERAL FACTS

Chapter 29

Factual Anecdotes and Monumental Cock-ups

A funeral should be the last memorable occasion of someone's life, and although people do not usually look forward to attending, it is important to make sure it will be remembered with the serenity and affection that it deserves.

If the majority of the mourners and family members are overheard saying "that was a really lovely service and it summed up Joe so well", then everyone will go home in reasonable spirits. But, as with organising any event, funerals can be subjected to mishaps. What makes it more raw than usual is the pent-up emotion associated with the passing of any loved one. The funeral director and his team may have done everything correctly from the moment their client walked into the office. Even up to the point where a family is collected from their home and travel en route to the chapel.

But major, monumental cock-ups do not include a puncture and a swift wheel change on the side of the road. Incidents such as these are comparatively easy to overcome and soon forgotten. Other situations are just impossible to rectify and beyond belief. The examples that follow are among the worst:

The Funeral Director Transports The Wrong Body
Enfield Independent 11th June 2013

Funeral staff were suspended at the Hertford Road branch of the Co-operative Funeralcare after a person who was supposed to be cremated was buried. The mix-up apparently occurred when the coffins were placed next to each other whilst preparing for the funerals.

Staff realised they had the wrong body when they came to do the second funeral which was then postponed. A spokesman for the Co-operative Funeralcare said:

"Regrettably, we can confirm that as a result of human error, the wrong deceased was buried at a cemetery in Enfield." Two members of staff were suspended whilst investigations were carried out.

Wrong Body Cremated
Mail online 8th February 2013

Two members of staff were sacked from the Co-operative Funeralcare when the wrong body had been cremated, which meant that a family and mourners turned up to the funeral of their loved one not realising that the coffin contained a complete stranger. The second family was forced to hold their funeral without the body as their relative had already been cremated.

The mix-up occurred when the wrong body was placed in a coffin and taken to Birtley Crematorium in Gateshead where the funeral took place. The error was discovered later when staff were preparing for another funeral. The family was informed that their loved one had already been cremated and the funeral had to proceed without the body.

Wrong Body in the Chapel of Rest
Wirral Globe 28th January 2009

A widower went to pay his last respects to his wife at the Co-operative Funeralcare in Wallasey and was devastated to discover that the wrong woman had been placed in the coffin, but dressed in his wife's funeral clothes. The gentleman was further distressed when funeral staff said that he was mistaken, insisting that the deceased woman in the coffin was his partner of 41 years. His wife had undergone chemotherapy treatment for cancer and as a result had lost her hair. The woman in the coffin had a full head of hair.

To make matters worse, a member of staff approached the gentleman with an envelope containing a pair of earrings just before he entered the chapel of rest, apologising that they were unable to put them on his wife. This had been specifically requested before she passed away as she had worn them for their son's wedding in Mauritius, but the woman in the coffin had not had her ears pieced.

Funeral Turns to Farce as Rival Undertaker Snatches Hearse Keys on Way to Burial
Mail online 13th May 2009

A Hartlepool woman's dying wish was to be taken to her final resting place in a classic Rolls Royce. The Phantom V1 owned by Irene Jessop Funeral Service sat in solemn silence to carry the coffin to the cemetery, and it became clear that someone had sabotaged the woman's final event, in the most callous way.

The hearse driver discovered that the keys had been taken out of the ignition, and in front of the family, the undertakers had to remove the dashboard and hotwire the car to get it started. Finally, they set off – an hour late. The culprit was later discovered to be David Wood, a rival undertaker.

Bradford Burglar Makes a Grave Mistake at Funeral Director's
Telegraph & Argus 22nd November 2013

A Slovakian man, who made a grave mistake when he mistook a funeral director's premises for a mobile phone shop, was convicted of burglary after overwhelming evidence.

Tibor Horvath, 22, was convicted of burglary after the Crown's barrister, Nadim Bashir, produced photos of the premises. The man was arrested for entering the adjoining flat of Ummah Funeral Service, supposedly to either fix the broken pieces of the mobile phone that was in his possession at the time, or to sell them. He claimed he was trying to sell them. But the barrister claimed that his story about thinking he was entering a mobile phone shop was a "cock and bull" story to get him off a charge of burglary.

He produced photographs of the business to the jury, showing headstones displayed outside, and said that the large sign saying 'Funeral Services' must have been a "dead giveaway".

Horse- Drawn Carriage Carrying a Coffin to a Funeral Overturns
The Telegraph 16th October 2008

Mourners watched in disbelief as the 100 year old hearse hit a bollard, causing it to veer into two cars before turning over onto the pavement. The coffin became dislodged inside the smashed antique carriage.

The horseman and two grooms were hurled to the ground during the incident in Ipswich when a car overtook the funeral service too quickly, causing the carriage to veer. Two of the four-team horses broke free and galloped down the street, damaging cars along the way.

The body was transferred to another hearse and taken to St Mary the Virgin church in Bramford. The service began two hours late.

The horseman, Mike Daniell, suffered an injured hip, and his son, Ed, suffered a broken nose and injured pelvis.

Mr Daniell said, "I have been taking horse-drawn funerals for 28 years and this is the first accident we have had. It was just a set of very unfortunate circumstances. There was no real spooking of the horses."

Horses Pulling Carriage Which Carried Murder Victim Thomas Thomson to His Funeral Spark Traffic Chaos After Bolting
Liverpool Echo 26th May 2011

A horse-drawn hearse, carrying the coffin of a murder victim, created havoc when the horses got spooked, dragging the hearse into parked cars before the horses broke free and bolted. They continued on through red traffic lights, causing cars to swerve, but thankfully nobody was injured. A motorised hearse was located nearby and the funeral was able to continue for the rest of the journey, arriving on time, with over 300 mourners waiting to pay their last respects.

Glasgow Funeral Staff Scammed Grieving Families
BBC News Glasgow and West Scotland 16ᵗʰ August 2013

Three funeral parlour workers at T & R O'Brien funeral home in Mayhill, owned by Dignity plc., were given community order sentences for defrauding grieving families. The women issued false invoices with inflated prices to families paying by cash. Coffins were overcharged by £500 and the proceeds were split between among the women.

Family in Shock As 'Murdered' Brazilian Man Turns Up At His Own Wake
The Independent 24ᵗʰ October 2012

A family in the Brazilian town of Alagoinhas had the shock of their lives when a relative they thought had been murdered turned up to his own wake. Family members fainted as others ran off in shock as the 41 year old car washer approached the group, gathered around a coffin containing what they thought was his body. The mistake occurred when a fellow car washer, said to closely resemble the family member, was murdered. His brother attended the mortuary and wrongly identified the man, as he had not seen his brother for months.

The 'Fake' at Mandela's Memorial – Interpreter Said it All
The Guardian 18ᵗʰ December 2013

Thamsaqa Jantjie claimed an 'attack of schizophrenia' rendered his signing unintelligible, but his performance translated an underlying truth. Standing alongside world leaders, including Barack Obama, was a rounded black man in formal attire, translating the service into sign language. Those versed in sign language gradually became aware that something strange was going on: the man was a fake and was making up his own signs; he was flapping his hands around, but there was no meaning in it.

A day later, the official inquiry disclosed that the 34 year-old was a qualified interpreter hired by the African National Congress from his firm South African Interpreters. In an interview with the Johannesburg newspaper *The Star*, Jantjie put his behaviour down to a sudden attack of schizophrenia, for which he takes medication: he had been hearing voices and hallucinating. "There was nothing I could do. I was alone in a very dangerous situation. I tried to tell the world what was going on. I am very sorry."

Chapter 30

Why the Funeral Industry is Preparing for a Surge in the Death Rate

Of course the massive increase in population accounts for a lot of this growth, but the increase of certain diseases has catalysed this currently.

The Rise of Cancer

Every human body contains more than a hundred trillion cells, and cells are the basic units of life. There are numerous types of cell within our bodies that continue to grow and divide, which produce more cells to keep us healthy.

They naturally replace the cells that have become old, or those that have died, but every now and then this natural process goes wrong. When the DNA of a cell becomes damaged or mutilated, it affects the normal process of cell division and growth. When this happens cells do not die when they should and new cells form where they are not needed, resulting in a mass of tissues called a tumour. Tumours are either benign (non-cancerous) or malignant (cancerous). These cells invade nearby cells and sometimes metastasise to other parts of the body.

All cancers begin inside cells, of which there are five different cancer groups and over 200 varieties of cancer that could strike a person at any given time.

These days many primary cancers can be treated with medication or surgery, but it is usually a secondary cancer that proves to be fatal, and not the primary one. Cancers tend to be more aggressive in younger people and slower growing in the elderly.

Cancer is developing faster than the drugs that treat it.

Poor Diet, Obesity and Related Disease

There have been some recent examples of people living past 100, such as Jeanne Calmant from France, who lived until she was 122 years and 164 days. Although the advance of modern drugs has helped prolong life.

According to government statistics, there were nine times more deaths with a primary diagnosis of obesity in 2012-13 as there was in 2002-03.

This year, the number of people diagnosed with diabetes reached 3.2 million. This sharp rise shows no sign of slowing down.

Chapter 31

Anatomical Facts & Funeral Statistics

Ask any funeral director; embalmer; mortician, coroner's office and they will say that:

- Approximately 500,000 to 600,000 deaths occur in Great Britain every year.
- The average human heart beats approximately 100,000 times a day and more than two and a half billion times by the time a person celebrates their 70th birthday.
- Why do most people hate Mondays? You are more likely to die of a heart attack on a Monday (according to a 10 year survey conducted in Scotland).
- Over 90% of diseases are caused as a result of stress.
- Your cremated remains will weigh approximately nine pounds.

Glossary of Terms

In artículo mortis:	at the point of death
Cremfilm:	coffin lining
Catafalque:	a decorative framework supporting a coffin during a funeral service
Committal:	the burial of a dead body; interment of cremated remains
Cortege:	a solemn procession, especially for a funeral
Homeostasis:	the tendency towards a relatively stable equilibrium between interdependent elements maintained by physiological processes
Hominidae:	modern man and extinct immediate ancestors of man
Interment:	the act or ritual of interring or burying
Intubate:	(embalming) the raising of a blood vessel
Polytainer:	plastic container for cremated remains
Tempus fugit:	time flies
Urn:	a rounded vase with a stem or a base for storing ashes of a cremated person

Image accreditations and special thanks:

Bellacouche
A Wakelin, WHEELS Midland Red Collection
Motorcycle Funerals Ltd
The Britannia Shipping Company for burials at sea
Drayhorse Shires
Irvin Amusements Ltd
The Celebrant Society www.celebrantsociety.org.uk
J S Professional Management Services Ltd
Funeral Flowers Network

Forms

1. Death Certificate
2. Your Instructions For Cremated Remains
3. Application For Permission To Erect A Monument
4. Application For Cremation Of The Body Or A Person Who Has Died
5. Medical Certificate

FORM 1: Death Certificate

DEATH	Entry No.

Registration district	Administrative area.

Sub District

1. Date and Place of Death

2. Name and Surname	3. Sex
	4. Maiden Surname of woman who married

5. Date and Place of Birth

6. Occupation and usual address

7.(a) Name and Surname of informant	(b) Qualification

(C) Usual address

8. I certify that the Particulars given by me above are true to the best of my knowledge and belief

Signature
of informant

9. Cause of death

10. Date of registration	11. Signature of registrar

Certified to be a true copy of an entry in a register in my custody

----

* Superintendent Registrar   Date

* Registrar

* Strike out whichever does not apply

CAUTION THERE ARE OFFENCES RELATING TO FALSIFYING OR ALTERING CERTIFICATE AND USING OR POSSESSING FALSE CERTIFICATE © CROWN COURT COPY

WARNING: A CERTIFICATE IS NOT EVIDENCE OF IDENTITY

FORM 2: Your Instructions for Created Remains:

YOUR INSTRUCTIONS FOR THE CREMATED REMAINS
IMPORTANT INFORMATION – PLEASE READ CAREFULLY

We would like to ask for your instructions for the final resting place of the ashes. Please remember, once the ashes have been scattered or buried, you will be unable to change your mind. If you are unsure, or if you are in any doubt what you would like to do, we strongly advise you postpone your decision to a later date.

We look after the ashes for you at the crematorium free of charge.

If you have decided what you would like to happen to the ashes

Please fill in the following information

All metal residues will be recycled by a non-profit making company

Please note that this form, filled in and signed by you, is written instructions to us, and we act on this accordingly.

Please complete in block capital letter:

I _____

Of address _____

_____

Telephone No. _____

Applicant for the cremation of _____

I instruct the crematorium manager to: Tick one

A)   Look after the ashes at the crematorium until I have made a final decision.
     (We will write to you after one month regarding your choice)

B)   Allow the funeral director or _____collect the ashes
     (Ashes can be returned to the crematorium at any time without charge)

C)   Place the ashes, Unwitnessed in the garden of remembrance
     **(Please note, it is important that you have time to reflect on this decision, so we will
     Contact you to confirm your instructions)**

D)   Please the ashes, witnessed in the garden of remembrance
     **(Please contact us to arrange a convenient date and time, If we are not contacted within
     3 months the ashes will be laid to rest as per the cremation regulations 1930 reg 16)**

E)   Please the ashes unwitnessed/witnessed with the late (insert name_____

Cremation Number _____ Location _____

I confirm I have read and understood the options available to me

I wish to reclaim the metal residues

Signature of Applicant _____ Date_____

Application to erect a monument

(Any Local Authority)
address and telephone number details

Form 3: Application For Permission To Erect A Monument

APPLICATION FOR PERMISSION TO ERECT A MONUMENT

In the _____ burial ground

I/we hereby apply for erection of a Monument in the above Burial Ground in accordance with the following particulars, and of the design and dimensions shown in the two attached drawings. The Council's approval of an inscription proposed to be made on the above Monument, copy of which is given below, is also sought.

In all cases the consent of the owner of a purchased grave is required before permission can be given by the Council for the erection thereon of a Monument. The following declaration is required to be signed in connection with the application.

I declare that I am the owner of the Exclusive Right of Burial in the above grave space and hereby make or consent to the application for the erection of a Monument. In accordance with current regulations.

- Check that your preferred stonemason is allowed to operate in a designated cemetery
- Compare memorial prices for marble and granite
- Consider the durability of the product
- Ask how much the cemetery permit fees are

Form 4: Application For Cremation Of The Body Or A Person Who Has Died

Application for cremation of the body of a person who has died

Cremation 1
replacing Form A

This form can only be completed by a person who is at least 16 years of age.
Please complete this form in full, if a part does not apply enter 'N/A'.

Part 1 Details of the crematorium

Name of crematorium where cremation will take place

Name of funeral director

Telephone number

Part 2 Your details (the applicant)

Your full name

Address

Telephone number

Part 3 Details of the person who has died

Full name

Address

Occupation or last occupation if retired or not in work at date of death

continued over the page ⇨

Regulation 16(1)(a) of the Cremation (England and Wales) Regulations 2008

It's Your Funeral

Part 3 continued

Age at date of death

Sex
☐ Male ☐ Female

Status
☐ married/civil partnership ☐ widow/widower/surviving civil partner ☐ Single

Part 4 The application

1. Are you a near relative or an executor of the person who has died? ☐ Yes ☐ No

Near relative means the widow, widower or surviving civil partner of the person who has died, or a parent or child of the person who has died, or any other relative usually residing with the person who has died.

If No, please give the nature of your relationship and explain why you are making the application rather than a near relative or an executor.

2. Is there any near relative(s) or executor(s) who has not been informed of the proposed cremation? ☐ Yes ☐ No

If Yes, please give the name(s) and the reason(s) why they have not been contacted.

3. Has any near relative or executor expressed any objection to the proposed cremation? ☐ Yes ☐ No

If Yes, please give details.

4. What was the date and time of death of the person who has died?

Date ☐☐/☐☐/☐☐☐☐

Time

continued over the page ☞

Cremation 1

2

Forms

Part 4 continued

5. Please give the address where the person died.

Address

[ ] [ ] [ ] [ ] [ ] [ ] [ ]

Please state whether it was the residence of the person who has died or a hotel, hospital, or nursing home etc.

[ ] Their home   [ ] Hospital   [ ] Other (please specify)

[ ] Hotel   [ ] Nursing home

6. Do you know or suspect that the death of the person who has died was violent or unnatural?   [ ] Yes   [ ] No

7. Do you consider that there should be any further examination of the remains of the person who has died?   [ ] Yes   [ ] No

If you have answered Yes to questions **6** or **7**, please give reasons below.

8. What is the name, address and telephone number of the usual doctor of the person who has died?

Doctor's name

Address   Telephone number

[ ] [ ] [ ] [ ] [ ] [ ] [ ]

It's Your Funeral

Part 5 Inspection of certificates

You are entitled to inspect the certificates (if any) given by doctors under regulation 16(c)(i) of the Cremation Regulations 2008 (forms Cremation 4 and Cremation 5). If you do not wish to inspect any such certificates yourself you may nominate another person to inspect them instead of you.

Such certificates will only be available for inspection at the offices of the cremation authority for **48 hours** from the time that the cremation authority notifies you, or the person you have nominated, that the certificates are available to be inspected. You may take someone with you when you attend to inspect the certificates. If you, or the person nominated by you, do not attend to inspect the certificates at the time agreed with the cremation authority, the cremation may then proceed.

Please state if you would like to inspect the certificates given by the doctors or whether you would like to nominate someone else to do so instead and give a contact telephone number.

If certificates are given by medical practitioners:-

☐ I would like to inspect the certificates and

my contact telephone number is _____

☐ I nominate _____

to inspect the certificates and their
contact telephone number is _____

Part 6 Statement of truth

I apply for the body of the person who has died to be cremated and I certify that I am at least 16 years of age.

I believe that the facts given in this application are true. I am aware that it is an offence to wilfully make a false statement with a view to obtaining the cremation of any human remains.

Print your full name
_____

Signed
_____

Dated
☐☐/☐☐/☐☐☐☐

Forms

Form 5: Medical Certificate

Cremation 4
replacing Form B

01.09

Medical certificate

This form can only be completed by a registered medical practitioner.
Please complete this form in full, if a part does not apply enter 'N/A'.

Part 1 Details of the deceased

Full name

Address

Occupation or last occupation if retired or not in work at the date of death

Where a past occupation of the deceased person may suggest that the death was due to industrial disease, you should consider whether to refer the death to a coroner.

Part 2 The report on the deceased

1. What was the date and time of death of the deceased?

Date ☐☐/☐☐/☐☐☐☐

Time

2. Please give the address where the deceased died.

Address

Please state whether it was the residence of the deceased or a hotel, hospital, or nursing home etc.

☐ Their home   ☐ Hospital   ☐ Other (please specify)

☐ Hotel   ☐ Nursing home

continued over the page ⇨

Regulation 16(c)(i) of the Cremation (England and Wales) Regulations 2008

It's Your Funeral

3. Are you a relative of the deceased?

☐ Yes ☐ No

If Yes, please give the nature of your relationship.

4. Have you, so far as you are aware, any pecuniary interest in the death of the deceased?

☐ Yes ☐ No

If Yes, please give details.

5. Were you the deceased's usual medical practitioner?

☐ Yes ☐ No

If Yes, please state for how long.

If No, please give details of your medical role in relation to the deceased.

6. Please state for how long you attended the deceased during their last illness?

7. Please state the number of days and hours before the deceased's death that you last saw them alive?

Days

Hours

8. Please state the date and time that you saw the body of the deceased and the examination that you made of the body.

Date ☐☐ / ☐☐ / ☐☐☐☐

Time

Examination

continued over the page ⇨

Forms

Part 2 continued

9. From your medical notes, and the observations of yourself and others immediately before and at the time of the deceased's death, please describe the symptoms and other conditions which led to your conclusions about the cause of death.

10. If the deceased died in a hospital at which they were an in-patient, has a hospital post-mortem examination been made or supervised by a registered medical practitioner of at least five years' standing who is neither a relative of the deceased nor a relative of yours or a partner or colleague in the same practice or clinical team as you? ☐ Yes ☐ No

If Yes, are the results of that examination known to you? ☐ Yes ☐ No

Note: 'Five years' standing' means a medical practitioner who has been a fully registered person within the meaning of the Medical Act 1983 for at least five years and, if paragraph 10 of Schedule 1 to the Medical Act 1983 (Amendment) Order 2002 (S.I. 2002/3135) has come into force, has held a licence to practice for at least five years or since the coming into force of that paragraph.

continued over the page ◄▷

3

183

It's Your Funeral

Part 2 continued

11. Please give the cause of death

1. (a) Disease or condition directly leading to death (this does not mean the mode of dying, such as heart failure, asphyxia, asthenia, etc: it means the disease, injury, or complication which caused death)

(b) Other disease or condition, if any, leading to (a)

(c) Other disease or condition, if any, leading to (b)

2. Other significant conditions contributing to the death but not related to the disease or condition causing it.

12. Did the deceased undergo any operation in the year before their death? ☐ Yes ☐ No

If Yes, what was the date and nature of the operation and who performed it.

Date of operation

☐☐/☐☐/☐☐☐☐

Who performed it

Nature of operation

13. Do you have any reason to believe that the operation(s) shortened the life of the deceased? ☐ Yes ☐ No

If Yes, please give details.

continued over the page ➩

Forms

Part 2 continued

14. Please give the full name and address details of any person who nursed the deceased during their last illness (Say whether professional nurse, relative, etc. If the illness was a long one, this question should be answered with reference to the period of four weeks before the death.)

[ ]

15. Were there any persons present at the moment of death? ☐ Yes ☐ No

If Yes, please give the full name and address details of those persons and whether you have spoken to them about the death.

[ ]

16. If there were persons present at the moment of death, did those persons have any concerns regarding the cause of death? ☐ Yes ☐ No

If Yes, please give details

[ ]

17. In view of your knowledge of the deceased's habits and constitution do you have any doubts whatever about the character of the disease or condition which led to the death? ☐ Yes ☐ No

18. Have you any reason to suspect that the death of the deceased was

Violent ☐ Yes ☐ No

Unnatural ☐ Yes ☐ No

19. Have you any reason at all to suppose a further examination of the body is desirable? ☐ Yes ☐ No

If you have answered Yes to questions **17**, **18** or **19** please give details below:

[ ]

continued over the page ⇨

Cremation 4

5

It's Your Funeral

20. Has a coroner been informed about the death? ☐ Yes ☐ No

If Yes, please state the outcome.

21. Has there been any discussion with a coroner's office about the death of the deceased? ☐ Yes ☐ No

If Yes, please state the coroner's office that was contacted and the outcome of the discussions.

22. Have you given the certificate required for registration of death? ☐ Yes ☐ No

If No, please give the full name and contact details of the medical practitioner who has

Full name

Address   Telephone number

23. Was any hazardous implant placed in the body (e.g. a pacemaker, radioactive device or 'Fixion' intramedullary nailing system)? ☐ Yes ☐ No

Implants may damage cremation equipment if not removed from the body of the deceased before cremation and some radioactive treatments may endanger the health of crematorium staff.

If Yes, has it been removed? ☐ Yes ☐ No

continued over the page ▷

186

Forms

Part 3 Statement of truth

I certify that I am a registered medical practitioner.

I certify that the information I have given above is true and accurate to the best of my knowledge and belief and that I know of no reasonable cause to suspect that the deceased died either a violent or unnatural death or a sudden death of which the cause is unknown or in a place or circumstance which requires an inquest in pursuance of any Act.

I am aware that it is an offence to wilfully make a false statement with a view to procuring the cremation of any human remains.

Your full name

Address

Telephone number

Registered qualifications

GMC Reference number

Signed

Dated ☐☐ / ☐☐ / ☐☐☐☐

Once completed, this certificate must be handed or sent in a closed envelope by, or on behalf of, the medical practitioner who signs it to the medical practitioner who is to give the confirmatory medical certificate except in a case where question 10 is answered in the affirmative, in which case the certificate must be so handed or sent to the medical referee at the cremation authority at which the cremation is to take place.

Confirmatory medical certificate

This form may only be completed by a registered medical practitioner of at least five years' standing who is not either a relative of the deceased, the medical practitioner who issued the medical certificate (form Cremation 4) or a relative or a partner or colleague in the same practice or clinical team as the medical practitioner who issued that certificate.

'Five years' standing' means a medical practitioner who has been a fully registered person within the meaning of the Medical Act 1983 for at least five years and, if paragraph 10 of Schedule 1 to the Medical Act 1983 (Amendment) Order 2002 (S.I. 2002/3135) has come into force, has held a licence to practice for at least five years or since the coming into force of that paragraph.

Please complete this form in full, if a part does not apply enter 'N/A'.

Part 1 Details of the deceased

Full name

Address

Occupation or last occupation if retired or not in work at the date of death

Part 2 The report on the deceased

1. Have you questioned the medical practitioner who gave the Medical Certificate (form Cremation 4)?

☐ Yes ☐ No

If No, please give reasons.

continued over the page ➪

Regulation 16(c)(i) of the Cremation (England and Wales) Regulations 2008

188

Forms

Part 2 continued

In answer to questions 2, 3, 4, and 5, please give names and addresses of persons questioned and say whether you spoke to them in person or by telephone. Any failure to answer one of these questions in the affirmative may be treated as inadequate enquiry.

2. Have you questioned any other medical practitioner who attended the deceased? ☐ Yes ☐ No

   If Yes, please give the full name and address details of the medical practitioner(s).

3. Have you questioned any person who nursed the deceased during their last illness, or who was present at the death? ☐ Yes ☐ No

   If Yes, please give the full name and address details.

4. Have you questioned any of the relatives of the deceased? ☐ Yes ☐ No

   If Yes, please give the full name and address details.

5. Have you questioned any other person? ☐ Yes ☐ No

   If Yes, please give the full name and address details.

continued over the page ⇨

It's Your Funeral

Part 2 continued

6. Please state the date and time that you saw the body of the deceased and the examination that you made of the body.

Date

☐☐ / ☐☐ / ☐☐☐☐

Time

Examination

7. Do you agree with the cause of death given in question 11 of Part 2 of the Medical Certificate (form Cremation 4)?   ☐ Yes   ☐ No

If No, please give reasons and give the cause of death.

Reason(s) for disagreeing

1. (a) Disease or condition directly leading to death (this does not mean the mode of dying, such as heart failure, asphyxia, asthenia, etc: it means the disease, injury, or complication which caused death)

   (b) Other disease or condition, if any, leading to (a)

   (c) Other disease or condition, if any, leading to (b)

2. Other significant conditions contributing to the death but not related to the disease or condition causing it.

continued over the page ⇨

Forms

Part 3

Statement of truth

I certify that I am a registered medical practitioner of at least five years' standing and I am not a relative of the deceased, or a relative or a partner or colleague in the same practice or clinical team as the medical practitioner who has given the Medical Certificate (form Cremation 4).

I certify that the information I have given above is true and accurate to the best of my knowledge and belief and that I know of no reasonable cause to suspect that the deceased died either a violent or unnatural death or a sudden death of which the cause is unknown or in a place or circumstance which requires an inquest in pursuance of any Act.

I am aware that it is an offence to wilfully make a false statement with a view to procuring the cremation of any human remains.

Your full name

Address

Telephone number

Registered qualifications

GMC reference number

Signed

Dated

Once completed, this certificate and the Medical Certificate (form Cremation 4) must be handed or sent in a closed envelope by one of the medical practitioners giving the certificates to the medical referee at the cremation authority at which the cremation is to take place.

Cremation 5

4

Printed in Great Britain
by Amazon